Agility
Fun The
Hobday
Way

D1607187

Written by Ruth Hobday

Volume II: Steps for Obstacle Training

Clean Run Productions   35 Walnut Street, Turners Falls, MA 01376

Published by Clean Run Productions
35 Walnut Street, Turners Falls, MA 01376-2317
Phone 413-863-9243 or 1-800-311-6503
Fax 413-863-8303

Edited by Monica Percival
Proofread by Bud Houston and Linda Mecklenburg
Book Design and Typesetting by Leslie G. Perry
Cover Design by Leslie G. Perry
Cover Photo by Russell Fine Art of England
Illustrations by Rebecca Cheek
Photos by Sandra Russell, Monica Percival, Bill Newcomb, and Nancy Gyes
Printed by Hadley Printing Company, Inc.

ISBN 0-9653994-8-6 (Volume II)
ISBN 0-9653994-7-8 (Multiple Volume Set)

Printed in the United States of America

Dedication

This book is dedicated to Heidi,
Sealight Hurricane, one of the really great
Agility stars and my dog of a lifetime. She
has taught me such a lot and also given me two more
generations of super dogs. Retired now from Agility, she
is still my constant companion and best friend. Thank
you Heidi—I shall never forget you.

Table of Contents

About the Author

Ruth Hobday got her first dog, a Cocker Spaniel named Rusty, when she was 16. Ruth took Rusty to the local Obedience Club and although he never became very obedient, her interest in dog training began.

A few years later she bought a Sheltie pup and decided to have a go at Obedience showing. Unfortunately Sheba, the Sheltie, was very nervous and always ran out of the stay exercise. Ruth noticed that several people worked two dogs and their dogs sat together in the Stays. So she began to train Kim, a rescue dog, so that Kim could keep Sheba company in the stays. Kim took to Obedience very well and quickly won out of Beginners and Novice. Ruth began to work the higher classes. Several years on and she was instructing and judging Obedience.

Ruth first got interested in Agility in 1979 soon after its invention. Once bitten by the Agility bug Ruth began to find that Agility took all her time.

Her first Agility dog was Riki, a large Sheltie. He did very well running both at Crufts and Olympia, but his achievements were quickly eclipsed when Heidi, Sealight Hurricane, came on the scene. She quickly became the top dog in the United Kingdom (U.K.) and stayed there for almost three years. It was during this time in 1987 that Ruth gave up her job as a Primary School teacher and began Hurricane Dog Training— named after Heidi, not the weather. This was a big step to take but she's never regretted it. Ruth comments, "I'll never get rich but I've got to see some of the world working in the U.S., Canada, Germany, Austria and Holland."

Ruth had written several Agility articles and a friend suggested that she write a book. *Agility is Fun Book 1* was published in

1989 and *Agility is Fun Book 2* followed in 1992. These books have sold well abroad as well as in the U.K. and have been translated into German.

In 1991 Ruth started to produce Agility training videos. These have been a great success and she now has seven different videos, covering all aspects of Agility training.

As well as doing training seminars, Ruth judges Agility and continues to compete. Heidi is twelve now and retired, although she still enjoys coming to shows and supervising the training of her children. At the moment Ruth is competing with Heidi's son and daughter, Tarka and Zany. They love Agility and have done very well. Tarka even managed to qualify for Olympia last year. Ruth also now has Dusky, daughter of Tarka, who is 13 months old and will hopefully follow in her Granny's footsteps.

Introduction

After writing *Agility is Fun Books 1 and 2,* I began to think
about writing a different type of Agility book. During my time
in Agility I have visited lots of different clubs. It seemed to me
that while most clubs could get beginners doing the equipment, it was the next stages where instruction was poor, and so
many handlers gave up before they had really started. Once a
dog can do the equipment he needs lots of practise of simple
exercises. Dogs and handlers become bored doing the same
thing and I felt that many instructors were really only steward-
ing, not instructing. I decided to write a set of training manuals with lots of lesson plans designed to help instructors with
their classes. Training manuals with structured plans from
beginners right through to advanced should give them plenty
of ideas and hopefully the confidence to make further plans
for themselves.

This then is the aim of *Agility Fun The Hobday Way.* Volume I
begins with puppy training and includes lesson plans for
puppy Agility classes. Here in Volume II, I am going to explain
the methods I use for introducing an adult dog to Agility.
There are several different ways to do this and I certainly don't
say that other ways are wrong. In Agility we are always learning and I teach some things very differently than I did in the
early days. These then are the methods I am using successfully
at the moment to introduce the various Agility obstacles.

The twelve-month-old puppies are now ready to join the older
dogs. After completing puppy classes, the pups' progress is
usually much quicker and smoother than the adult dogs just
beginning Agility. Also, hopefully, they will be so used to doing
obstacles that it will not be necessary to use the lead. This is
the big advantage of a puppy training program such as the one
described in Volume I.

Chapter One Teaching the Dog to Jump

Chapter One
Teaching the Dog to Jump

As all Agility courses contain a number of hurdles, it is essential that a dog enjoys jumping and is good and reliable at it. How then do we go about ensuring this is so? I feel that the way a dog is introduced to jumping is very important. In this chapter I am going to go through the entire sequence of teaching the dog to jump. Obviously, this will take several weeks or even months. In a later chapter I will explain how much I do in each lesson.

Most dogs jump naturally and many beginner handlers come to their first agility class saying "Oh I don't need to teach my dog to jump, he easily clears our 6 foot gate." Well that may be so, but the dog isn't jumping on command and a 6 foot gate looks very different than most Agility fences.

A lot of jumping faults seen in competition can be traced back to the way the dog was taught to jump. The temptation to get the dog jumping his full height as quickly as possible is great and many collies are quite capable of this even at their first lesson. However, lots of problems are caused by making the dog jump too high before he has acquired confidence in jumping. I see lots of dogs that run past or under hurdles, dogs that crash into hurdles not really attempting to clear them, and many dogs that hesitate, taking lots of little steps and gathering themselves before each hurdle. So many of these faults could have been prevented with a more careful introduction to jumping.

So how do I go about introducing the dog to jumping. In the years since I wrote *Agility is Fun Book 1*, I have altered my method of training slightly. At that time I taught the dog to jump using several poles on each hurdle and raising the height slowly until the dog could jump his full height. When I felt that the dog was confident enough, I lowered the height again and taught him to jump a single pole. However, I now use a single pole right from the beginning. I find this way you end up with a much more reliable jumper and single pole jumps rarely cause any problems.

I don't like to do any jumping with a dog before he is at least twelve months old. With heavy-boned breeds, such as the G.S.D., I advise waiting until the dog is fifteen to eighteen months old. The dog's bones need to be mature before he is asked to repeatedly take off and land.

This then is how I teach a dog to jump.

Standard Jumps

Since the dog will be working on the lead in the initial training, it is easier to use non-winged hurdles as wings tend to get in the way. Also, the handler can stay closer to the dog who is then less likely to run past the jump.

Commands

The most commonly used commands are JUMP, UP and OVER. Personally I prefer JUMP or UP as I find it hard to get "lift" in your voice when using OVER.

Equipment

Set out a straight line of three or four hurdles placed about 8 paces apart, each with a single pole set between 6 and 12 inches (a very tiny dog will need it lower still), depending on the height of the dog. If possible, use non-winged hurdles.

Training Notes

- I always use a row of hurdles so that the dog begins to realise that Agility obstacles are strung together and so that he doesn't get into the habit of stopping after each obstacle.

- I encourage handlers to use a toy as a reward, giving the dog a game at the end of the row of jumps.

- At this stage, always walk back to the start and don't let the dog come back over the jumps he has just done.

Stage 1

With the dog on the lead, (use a plain collar, not a choke collar) and working on the side the handler is most used to, get both the handler and the dog to jump the first hurdle. If this is successful let the handler and dog carry on over the other hurdles. There are several points to watch:

- Decide what command the handler is going to use and give this about a yard from the jump.

- Tell the handler to go steady—it isn't necessary to run at this stage.

- Remember to praise the dog after each jump but don't make a fuss if the dog runs by or pushes under. So many new handlers praise in the wrong place. Remember the dog lives in the present and praise given to reassure a dog who has run past a jump can be easily misinterpreted by the dog. If the dog goes wrong, don't tell him off—simply don't praise him. Do it again, and if successful give lots of praise.

Figure 1-1
Handler and dog go over the jumps together.

Figure 1-2
Working the dog on the right.

- Keep the lead fairly short so that it keeps the dog in the centre of the jump.

As soon as the handler and dog have successfully completed this, move on to Stage 2.

Stage 2
Place the dog on the handler's other side and repeat the row of hurdles with the handler still stepping over the poles with the dog. I find the earlier you start the dog working on both sides the better. However, just occasionally you may get a dog who has done so much work on the left that he gets very upset if asked to work the other side. Although having a dog that will work either side is really essential for Agility competition, it is not worth upsetting the dog at this stage. It is more important to get him jumping happily, then you may be able to try again to get him to work on the right. With the majority of dogs, however, there should be no problem.

Once the dog is happily doing Stages 1 and 2, go on to Stage 3.

Stage 3
Repeat Stage 1, but now with the handler keeping to the side of the hurdles.

Stage 4
Repeat Stage 3 with the handler working the dog on the other side.

This is all I try to achieve in the first lesson. The number of times you do the line of jumps depends on the individual dog. It is important to keep the dog happy and stop before he gets bored or tired. Some dogs may need to repeat this first lesson at their next Agility session, but the majority will be able to progress to the next lesson.

Early Jumping Practise
I feel that with a beginner dog it is very important to get forward movement and encourage the dog to look ahead for the next obstacle before beginning to teach the sharp turns that will be necessary later. With this in mind, all early jumping practice is done over straight lines of jumps or large circles.

I encourage the handler to try without the lead as soon as possible, but I am always prepared to put the lead back on if the dog starts to run past jumps. How soon you can manage without the lead often depends on how good the handler's general control is. It often helps for the handler to go back to jumping the hurdles with the dog when first removing the lead.

Figure 1-3
Now the handler runs at the side of the hurdles, working the dog on both sides.

Increasing the Height

The height of the jumps will depend on each dog's progress. I move the height up fairly slowly until it is about 6 inches below the dog's full height. I then leave the dog at this height for several weeks or even months until he is really confident at jumping.

The Long Jump

Once a dog is really happy jumping 6 inches lower than his full height, I introduce him to spread-type jumps. By now most dogs will be capable of jumping the full height; however, before asking them to do this I get them used to stretching over spread jumps. I feel that this helps them to gain confidence and hopefully a good style of jumping before tackling full height. The first spread the dog meets is the long jump.

How I set out the long jump depends on the size of the dog. For big dogs, the maximum Agility long jump is only 5 feet long and doesn't present much of a problem to the average collie or G.S.D., so I leave the boards horizontal. I start with three or four boards, depending on their width (an overall jump length of about 30 inches is best). With mini dogs or less agile big dogs, I always start with the boards on their sides so that it is less inviting for the dog to step on the boards. With very small dogs, I only use two boards with an overall length of about 1 foot.

Figure 1-4
Reward the dog with a game after each stage of jump training.

With all dogs I put a low hurdle in the middle of the long jump. There are two reasons for this: 1) the dog has learned how to jump ordinary hurdles and therefore will expect to jump; and 2) the hurdle helps the dog jump higher, thus making it easier for him to achieve the length. The height of this hurdle again depends on the dog's height. I suggest 15-18 inches for big dogs and 8-10 inches for mini dogs.

Commands

I always recommend using a different command for a long jump than the command for ordinary hurdles (usually LONG or BIG). The reason for this is that on a course you may find an ordinary hurdle quite close to a long jump. If the handler has only one command for all jumps, he must not be upset if the dog does the wrong obstacle. I have also found that many dogs, including my own, don't think of a long jump as much of an obstacle, and given the chance they will often choose something else. By having a different command, I feel that the odds are more in the handler's favour of having the dog perform the obstacle. When first introducing the dog to the long jump, I do have handlers use their ordinary jump command because the dog already knows it. It is easy to change later—just tag the new command on the end for a while, then leave out the old one.

Figure 1-5
A low hurdle helps the dog jump higher over the long jump.
Artist: Rebecca Cheek

Figure 1-6
Once the dog is happy with the long jump, placing a hurdle after the long jump encourages the dog to go on.
Artist: Rebecca Cheek

Training Notes

- When training the long jump it is important to vary the direction that the handler and dog turns after completing the obstacle. Many handlers, if left alone, will always turn to the right after the jump. Their dogs soon begin to cross jump in anticipation of the turn.

- In training, I often put an ordinary hurdle about 6 paces in front of the long jump so that the dog approaches it at speed. The dog is then less likely to suddenly refuse.

- As with all training, always remember the praise

- As soon as the dog is happy jumping the long jump, I put an ordinary hurdle after it. This encourages the dog to go on after the long jump and not begin stopping and turning to see where his handler is—problems that can cause the dog to start cross jumping this obstacle.

Stage 1

Introduce the dog to this new obstacle on the lead. I find it best if the handler jumps *with* the dog the first time. This prevents the dog from going past at the side, as long as the handler keeps the lead fairly taut. With the hurdle in the middle there is no need for corner poles, so there is nothing to catch the lead on. If a handler does not want to jump with the dog, he must hold the lead out over the jump to keep the dog in the middle.

Figure 1-7
A water jump.
Photo by Russell Fine Art

As with any new obstacle, I always introduce it with the dog on the side he is happiest—for most dogs this will be on the handler's left. After the dog has done the obstacle a few times on this side, I get the handler to try working the dog on the other side. With dogs and handlers used to working both sides, this is no problem. However, there is always the odd dog that is so used to working only on the left, that he gets upset when asked to work on the right. In this case, I let the handler stick to the left side until the dog is quite happy with the obstacle—it is more important to keep the dog happy than to get him to work both sides right now.

As soon as possible the handler stops jumping and runs alongside the dog, being careful not to pull the dog to one side if still using the lead. As with every obstacle in Agility, I encourage handlers to remove the lead as soon as possible.

Stage 2

Once the dog is happily jumping this short long jump off the lead, begin to lengthen the jump. In the case of a mini dog, stand the boards upright. I keep the hurdle in the middle until the dog is doing his full length.

Stage 3

Finally, remove the hurdle and put the four corner poles in position.

Problems That May Occur

Clipping the first or last board: As the dog is faulted if he touches any part of this obstacle, it is vital that the dog clears the long jump with inches to spare. If your dog does get careless and begins to clip this obstacle, I recommend a few training sessions with the hurdle placed back in the middle. With big dogs I have even put the hurdle up to 24 inches. This makes the dog jump higher, and therefore longer, and usually cures the problem.

Walking on the planks: Dogs with this problem need retraining with the boards on their sides. Use the hurdle in the middle of the long jump as well to give extra height.

Water Jumps

A water jump is only a short long jump, so once the dog is confident with the long jump, try to give him the experience of a water jump. I use the same command as for the long jump.

Figure 1-8
An ascending double spread.

Figure 1-9
A triple spread.

Figure 1-10
The well
jump.
Photo by
Russell Fine
Art

Spread Jumps

Once the dog is proficient with the long jump I introduce spread jumps. What is an Agility spread? Basically it is two or three single jumps placed closely together to be jumped as a single hurdle. The feet of the side supports of the jumps should not be interlocking and the uprights should be in line. If two jumps are used, it is called a double spread and if three jumps are used, it is called a triple spread. (In the U.S., you will sometimes see specially built doubles and triples that are a single unit rather than individual jumps.)

A double can be a parallel spread, meaning that both bars are set at identical heights. Alternatively, if the front bar is set at least 6 inches lower than the second bar, it is called an ascending spread. An ascending double is now the only type of spread jump allowed in the U.K. and the length of the spread can be a maximum of 30 inches. In the U.S., the maximum length of the spread is dependent on the rules of a particular agility organization and it also varies for mini and open dogs. A triple spread is always ascending—the third bar is set at the dog's jump height, the middle bar is lower, and the front bar is still lower.

In the U.K., spread jumps seem to go in and out of fashion in Agility; they are often used by some judges but rarely by others. In the winter, when there is less room in indoor riding

Figure 1-11
Building a spread jump over the long jump.

schools, they do not appear very often. The one class where spreads are often seen is Gamblers, where normally they are worth two points instead of one point as for ordinary hurdles. In the U.S. many courses contain a spread jump.

It is important that the Agility prospect experiences all types of spreads before he meets one in the ring. The well is another type of spread jump, and one that is often used in the U.K., so the dog should also learn about these. Teaching the well jump is discussed at the end of this chapter.

Commands
What command to use? I find it best to use my ordinary jump command, but perhaps add something to it to warn the dog that a spread is coming up. For example, if your jump command is UP, use GET UP; or if your jump command is OVER, use RIGHT OVER.

Training Notes
• As with training the long jump, it is important to vary the direction that the handler turns after a spread—don't let the dog begin to cross jump. I often set up three other jumps to form a square so that you can then vary what the dog does after the spread.

• When the dog is proficient at jumping ascending spreads, try a low parallel one with a spread of about 18 inches. It is even more vital with a parallel spread to have a low pole on the front hurdle. Even though parallel spreads are not allowed in

competition now in the U.K., I still teach the dog to jump them in training and as preparation for introducing the well.

• I don't increase the height or length of either type of spread jump any further until the dog can jump his full height over single hurdles.

• When running a course containing a spread, help the dog— particularly a beginner dog—by setting him up as straight as possible when tackling a spread. Some small dogs may always find a maximum spread a bit of an effort and this dog will need as much encouragement as possible. You can put a lot of encouragement into your voice if you try and it does help the dog.

Stage 1
I introduce the beginner dog to a low spread which I build *over* the first three boards of the long jump. There are two reasons for using the long jump in this way: 1) The dog has already learned how to stretch out over the long jump, which he will also need to do for the spread jump; 2) With all spread jumps, a ground line is a big help to the dog and there is no better ground line to start with than the long jump.

I start with an ascending spread—a bar at 12 inches and at 18 inches for big dogs; lower for the smaller dog. The first long jump board is just in front of the first hurdle. The spread from front to back is about 18 inches long for big dogs, about 12 inches long for smaller dogs. If possible, the handler has the

Figure 1-12
A brush fence.
Photo by Russell Fine Art

Figure 1-13
A bone jump.
Photo by Russell Fine Art

dog off lead right from the start with this obstacle; therefore, I prefer to use jumps with wings. Winged jumps make it less inviting for the dog to jump diagonally across the spread, (which puts him in danger of banging himself on the upright). If the handler has to use a lead, you will need to use jumps without wings. In this case, I would only let this dog jump low spreads until he is capable of working off lead.

Stage 2
Once the dog is happy jumping this low spread, remove the back two boards of the long jump. Then slowly increase the height of the hurdles until the dog is jumping an ascending spread with the back hurdle 6 inches below his full height.

Stage 3
If there are no problems, remove the remaining long jump board but replace it with a low pole on the front hurdle. Even in competition it is important to have a low pole on the first hurdle to give the dog a ground line.

Figure 1-14
A wall jump.
Photo by Russell Fine Art

Jumping Full Height
I never rush a dog into jumping his full height. I find if you wait until the dog is really confident and happy jumping 6 inches lower, he will hardly notice that extra 6 inches when you finally ask him to do it. So how do you get this confidence?

Lots of practise and encouragement over simple patterns of jumps. Give lots of praise for success and achieve forward movement before tackling tight turns.

Once the dog has realised that Agility obstacles are strung together, he will start to look for the next obstacle. I feel that it is extremely important to get this forward movement before teaching tight turns. It is so easy to actually teach a dog to circle and flap around in front of the handler, getting frustrated, getting in the way and wasting valuable time. Practising repeated sharp turns before the dog has the idea of forward movement quickly causes this fault.

Practising lots of straightforward jumping exercises and also send-aways over jumps will help to get the dog thinking and looking ahead. With the send-away it is important to give the dog something, such as a toy or tidbit, to aim at. I find using the table as the last obstacle very good as this is something big for the dog to see. You can also use the pause box. Whichever obstacle you use, you can bait it with a toy or tidbit to help encourage the dog to look ahead. If the dog has been trained to go to a bait tray, this can be placed on the table or in the pause box.

Once the dog is going ahead happily, looking for the next jump, then you can start doing more complicated jump patterns. These can easily be done at low heights. The handler then can concentrate on control without worrying about the height.

So don't be in a hurry to get the dog jumping full height. A lot of ground work done over lower jumps makes for a happy, confident jumper who will take full height in his stride. When I do finally decide the dog is ready to jump his full height I just put the odd jump up on a straightforward course and normally find that the dog sails over without even noticing the extra height. If necessary you can raise the height in 1 inch stages. Soon the dog will be happily jumping all the hurdles on the course at his full height. I will still continue to use a lower height for complicated exercises and I am always prepared to lower the height if for any reason the dog seems to lose his confidence.

Once the dog is jumping his full height it is important to give him lots of practise with all kinds of different looking hurdles—wall jumps, brush fences, bone jumps, and so on. I don't try a wall jump before the dog can jump full height happily because I don't want the dog to be tempted to stand on it.

The Well

I like a dog to be happy jumping full height and spreads before he attempts the well, which is so inviting for him to stand on. In competition a dog is faulted if he touches any part of this obstacle, so it is important for the dog to learn that he must jump through cleanly. Until a dog is really confident at jumping, I feel it is asking for trouble to put him at the well. A few weeks more training may make all the difference.

The first time you try this obstacle, make sure that you approach it with confidence; the dog may do it straight off. If the dog runs past at the side, put the lead on and try again, letting go of the lead as the dog jumps. Don't be too worried if the dog hesitates on take-off and puts a foot down on the well as he goes over. At least he has jumped, and often on the next attempt will jump through cleanly. If the dog still refuses, see if it is possible to remove the roof of the jump. Doing this makes the well look a lot less formidable. If the roof cannot be removed, try enticing the dog with a tidbit or his favourite toy. If all else fails, remove the pole and encourage the dog to jump up onto the base, maybe by getting the handler to sit on it. This is not to be recommended but I did have to resort to this once with a dog who was really frightened of the well. Once this dog had got over his initial fear we were able to continue training in the usual way.

If a dog persists in banking (standing on) the well, try the following: Place a white pole on the ground just in front of the obstacle and get someone to hold two more white poles, one on either side of the well pole, to make it look like an ascending spread. It is best if this person stands the opposite side to the handler. Experiment with these poles; if the dog is standing on the front, try holding both poles in front of the well pole, still keeping one lower than the other. Another thing that sometimes works is to stand a number of loose poles on the well body, if the dog stands on these and they fall off with a clatter, it may make him jump cleanly the next time. One thing you need to remember when working with the well, is that the dog will quickly get tired of it, particularly if he is not doing very well. Sometimes it is worth leaving it and trying again the next training session when the dog is nice and fresh.

When competing try to give the dog a good straight run at the well. If your dog is not too confident with this obstacle, be careful not to anticipate trouble yourself and let your anxiety show in your voice. Approach with confidence and all may be well. Finally remember the praise when the dog has done his best.

Tips for All Jump Training

It is important with all jumping training to keep the following points in mind.

- Keep your dog fit—never jump a lame dog or go on jumping if the dog is tired.

- Never over-face a dog. Be sure he is capable of the height before putting him at the hurdle.

- Always think about safety of the dog—be sure to put him straight at spreads and make sure he won't crash into another obstacle as he lands.

- Never be afraid to lower jumps if the dog loses his confidence or has had a long lay-off for some reason.

- Keep it fun and remember the praise.

Chapter Two The Contact Obstacles

Chapter Two
The Contact Obstacles

I have two different methods of introducing the contact obstacles. First, I shall explain how I do this with the inexperienced handler who is new to Agility. Later, I will describe the method I use with experienced, competitive handlers.

Commands

One of the first decisions the handler must make is whether to use a different command for each of the contact obstacles or whether to use the same command for all of them. It is fairly unusual to find contact obstacles very close together on a course so using the same command should rarely be a problem. Many handlers like to have a different command for the dog walk and the see-saw to warn the dog which one he is going up. I, myself, have always used the same command for these two obstacles and have never felt that the dog was confused. I think dogs are intelligent enough to tell the difference between these two obstacles, but I have no objections to handlers using different commands if they wish.

The most common commands are WALK ON, PLANK, CLIMB, and UP. Choose commands that are different from your other Agility commands.

Overview of Method 1

I use this method with handlers who are new to Agility or with handlers who never want to compete. With this method, the contact obstacles are taught one at a time, beginning with the A-frame (the easiest of the contact obstacles) and ending with the see-saw (the more difficult of the contact obstacles). Ideally the dog starts training on a lowered obstacle and works up to competition height. When the dog has mastered a particular obstacle, the next contact obstacle is introduced.

Basically, the handler leads the dog up and over the obstacle, all the way to the bottom. The handler praises the dog while he's still on the down contact and then releases the dog from the contact.

The A-Frame: Method 1 for Inexperienced Handlers

When introducing dogs to the contact obstacles, I do the A-frame first because I find that with most dogs it is the width of the plank that worries them a lot more than the height of the obstacle. If possible, the A-frame should be lowered until the apex is about 4 feet high. This, as well as making it easier to do, enables the handler to hold the dog as he goes over the top.

Stage 1

Working the dog on the side the handler is happiest and holding the dog by the collar rather than the lead, the handler should quietly walk the dog up and over the obstacle. By holding the collar the handler should be able to keep the dog in the middle of the obstacle. I always position myself on the opposite side of the obstacle, ready to assist if necessary. The chosen command for the obstacle should be used as the dog goes up the ramp and praise given as the dog reaches the down contact. Handlers should be encouraged to make the dog walk to the very bottom and to praise while the dog is still on the contact. Repeat several times if necessary.

Figure 2-1
The handler holds the dog by
the collar.
Artist: Rebecca Cheek

Figure 2-2
Walk the dog to the very
bottom.
Artist: Rebecca Cheek

Repeat Stage 1 working the dog on the other side.

Occasionally I get a dog that is very unsure on one side, usually the handler's right. In this case I let the handler stick to the better side until the dog is confident with the obstacle. With the majority of dogs, however, it is far better to work them on both sides right from the start. Using an A-frame that will lower has the added advantage that if you get a very nervous dog it is quite possible for the handler to walk over the obstacle with the dog, or to sit on the top and call the dog up. This needs to be done with care to ensure that the handler is not pushed off, and I find it rarely necessary.

Stage 2
Holding the lead now rather than the collar, the handler walks the dog over the obstacle making sure he goes to the bottom and prais-

ing while the dog is still on the contact. The handler must watch the dog carefully and be ready to push him back into the centre if he tries to jump off at the side. If a dog persists in jumping off the side, put two leads on him. With the instructor on the opposite side to the handler, keep both leads taut to prevent this from becoming a habit.

Repeat with the dog on the other side.

How many times it will be necessary to repeat Stage 2 will differ from dog to dog. It is important that the dog does not get tired or bored and after a couple of tries it may be necessary to do something else, returning to the A-frame later. If the dog is going over happily, it may be possible to raise the obstacle a little in this first lesson. Other dogs may need it low for a week or two.

Figure 2-3 (above)
With the A-frame at full height you still need to control the dog on the contact.

Figure 2-4 (right)
If you can't lower the A-frame use two leads to guide the dog.

Raising the A-Frame

Once the A-frame is raised it will be harder to keep the dog on the contact. Therefore, training for several weeks with the obstacle low and insisting that the dog waits on the contact, will hopefully form a habit that will make it easier to control the dog when the obstacle is raised to competition height. I usually raise it fairly quickly to a height of 5 feet, then leave it at this height until the handler has good control. Mini dogs often need a lowered A-frame for some weeks to enable them to gain the confidence necessary to get over the competition height A-frame. Never be afraid to lower the obstacle again if a dog loses his confidence.

If Your A-Frame Can't Be Lowered

If your A-frame is impossible to lower, it will be necessary to put two leads on the dog—the instructor holds one lead on one side of the A-frame and the handler holds the second on the opposite side of the obstacle. By keeping both leads taut it is possible to keep the dog in the centre of the A-frame. You may need a third person to give the dog a help from behind. However, it is much easier and kinder if you can lower the A-frame.

The Dog Walk: Method 1 for Inexperienced Handlers

As with the A-frame it is much easier if you can lower this obstacle before introducing it to the dog. I always start dogs on my puppy dog walk which is 12 inches wide and only 2 feet high.

If you can keep the dog moving on this obstacle you will have little trouble and most dogs are soon ready to move to the regulation dog walk. Remember to work this obstacle with the dog on both sides and as with the A-frame stop him and praise him on the down contact.

Stage 1

Working the dog on the side the handler is happiest and holding the dog by the collar rather than the lead, the handler should quietly walk the dog up and over the obstacle. By holding the collar, the handler should be able to keep the dog in the middle of the obstacle. I always position myself on the opposite side of the obstacle so that I can steady the dog if necessary. The chosen command for the obstacle should be used as the dog goes up the board and praise given as the dog reaches the down contact. Handlers should be encouraged to make the dog walk to the very bottom and to praise while the dog is still on the contact. Repeat several times.

Repeat Stage 1 working the dog on the other side.

Holding the lead now rather than the collar, the handler walks the dog over the obstacle again making sure he goes to the bottom and praising while the dog is still on the contact. The handler must watch the dog carefully and be very careful not to pull the dog off balance with the lead.

Repeat with the dog on the other side.

Figure 2-5
Remember to stop and praise the dog on the contact.

I do sometimes have difficulty when introducing this obstacle to large dogs. German Shepherds in particular often seem to have trouble controlling their hind legs. The problems start when the dog stops. His legs go rigid and he starts to wobble. If this happens, the handler should quietly reassure the dog for a few moments before trying to get him moving again. I often find that gently holding the base of the dog's tail will help to steady him. If at all possible, you should keep the dog from either jumping off or being lifted off by an anxious handler. It is far better to persuade the dog to complete the obstacle even if this takes a lot of help and time. Once the dog has finished the obstacle let him do something else for a while before trying the dog walk again.

If the dog is unhappy about walking up the plank and the handler is able to lift him, place the dog halfway up the down plank and teach him how to get off the plank before asking him to walk up it. Once he is happy doing the down plank, lift him onto the top plank and proceed from there. Work back in this way until the dog can do the whole obstacle.

How many times it will be necessary to repeat Stage 2 will differ from dog to dog. It is important that the dog does not get tired or bored and after a couple of tries it may be necessary to do something else, returning to the dog walk later.

Raising the Dog Walk
Once the dog is happily going over the lowered dog walk, gradually raise the height until he is doing the obstacle at competition height.

The Cross-Over: Method 1 for Inexperienced Handlers
This obstacle is rarely used in competition in the U.K. now. It is used more often in the U.S. and is a very useful obstacle in training. Dogs that are wary on the narrow top plank of the dog walk are often happier on the cross-over with its table-like top where they can rest and be reassured by their handler before starting the

Figure 2-6
The cross-over.

down plank. The cross-over is also an excellent obstacle for direction control training. I would not be without mine.

I introduce the cross-over in the same way as the dog walk. I position myself on the opposite side to the handler who holds the dog by the collar and encourages him to walk up the plank. Although it is not necessary for the dog to stop on top, I find that stopping the dog for a few moments allows the beginner handler time to reposition himself for the descent. At this stage I don't worry the beginner handler with direction commands, but the more experienced handler may want to use these right from the start. The command to turn needs to come just before the dog reaches the top. Remember to practise both turns, working the dog on the appropriate side.

The See-Saw: Method 1 for Inexperienced Handlers

I like a dog to be happy on the dog walk before he attempts a moving plank. Before asking him to walk up the see-saw, I get the handler to stand with the dog near the obstacle while I move the plank up and down a few times. Thus the dog sees that this plank moves and hears the noise it makes before he gets onto it, and is a lot less likely to confuse it with the dog walk.

Stage 1
With the dog on the side they are happiest (usually the handler's left), and holding him by the collar, the handler quietly walks the dog up to the centre point of the plank, and stops him in a WAIT. I position myself behind the handler and dog as they start forward, and once the dog has reached the centre and is steady, I slowly and smoothly lower the plank. Once the plank is on the ground, the handler moves the dog down to the contact. On the contact, the dog is praised before being given the release word which allows him to leave the see-saw.

Repeat this, then repeat with the dog on the other side.

Stage 2
I then show the handler how to hold the dog with the hand nearest to him and prevent the plank from banging down with the other hand.

It is important to make sure that the handler only stops the plank from banging down and doesn't hold it so tightly that he prevents

Figure 2-7
The instructor controls the plank.

Figure 2-8
Now the handler controls the plank.

Figure 2-9
The dog will soon learn to control the plank himself.

the dog from tipping it. The dog will quickly learn to control the tip himself if allowed. The first few times that a new handler controls the tip, I always stand close by to prevent the plank from banging down, should the handler get in a mess with his hands. As soon as possible the dog should be allowed to do this obstacle without being held. If still working on the lead, care must be taken so that the handler doesn't pull the dog off balance.

Once the beginner dog and handler have been introduced to all the contact obstacles, they need lots of simple control exercises to help them practise. I shall describe these in a later chapter.

Overview of Method 2

The aim of this second method of introducing the contact obstacles is to hopefully teach the dog to focus on the down contact, while getting there as quickly as possible. If you want to win in Agility these days, you do not have time to slow your dog on the contacts. However, it's no good having a fast dog over the obstacles if he misses the contact each time. I feel that this method, if taught correctly, teaches the dog that the best place to be on a contact obstacle is the down contact.

To use this method successfully the handler has to be prepared to put in a lot of work and repetition, which is why I don't use it with handlers new to Agility, or with handlers who never want to compete. With this method, all of the contact obstacles are taught at the

Figure 2-10
Place the dog on the down contact and praise.

Figure 2-11
*At full height
it is easier for
the dog to
have his
front feet on
the ground.*

same time. So you would do Stage 1 for all three contact obstacles until the dog is ready to move on to Stage 2. To make it easier to explain I shall work through all the stages for each obstacle in turn.

Commands

Before you begin, decide on a command for the down contact point—TIP, FEET, TOUCH or BOTTOM are some suggestions. The command I use is a drawn out OOOON. You also need a release command. This could be something like OK or it could be the command for the next obstacle. Use HEEL or CLOSE if you are not going onto another Agility obstacle.

The A-Frame: Method 2 for Experienced Handlers

To teach this method on the A-frame you need an adjustable one. If this is not available, introduce the dog walk and see-saw first. The A-frame should be set with the apex at about 3 feet.

Stage 1

Decide which side of the obstacle is to be the down contact. With the dog facing away from the obstacle, have the handler lift him up and place him, with all four feet, on this contact, giving his contact command as he does so. The handler should hold the dog here and praise lavishly, giving a tidbit if he wishes. The handler should

not use a WAIT command—the dog must learn to stop on the contact himself. After several seconds, have the handler give the release word and walk the dog off the obstacle.

Repeat this at least ten times during each training session, remembering to have the dog both on the right side as well as the left as the handler lifts him onto the obstacle.

Only move on to Stage 2 when the dog will wait on the contact without being held. This may take several training sessions.

Stage 2

With the dog on lead, have the handler pick him up and place him just above the down contact. Giving his contact command, the handler should walk the dog onto the contact and then praise and continue on as in Stage 1. At this stage with the A-frame, I allow the dog to walk down until his two front feet are on the ground. When the A-frame is at full height it will be much easier for him to stop with his front feet here than on the obstacle. It is important though that the front feet are only just on the ground and the rest of the dog is on the contact.

Figure 2-12
Now start the dog just below
the apex.

Repeat this many times with the handler working both sides until the dog will walk down and stop without being held. If he jumps off, simply have the handler pick him up and place him back on the contact, holding him as in Stage 1. The handler should say nothing as he puts the dog back, but then lavishly praise when the dog is on the contact and release the dog.

Slowly increase the height at which the dog is placed on the obstacle until he is doing Stage 2 from just below the apex.

Once the dog is reliable, slowly raise the height of the A-frame until the apex is set at about 4 feet, 6 inches.

Repeat Stage 2, working the dog *off the lead*.

Stage 3
Lower the A-frame again. With the dog on the lead, have the handler quietly walk him over the entire obstacle, stopping the dog on the contact as before.

Repeat many times, working the dog on both sides.

Stage 4
Repeat Stage 3 with the dog *off the lead*. Put the lead back on at any time, if it becomes necessary.

Repeat many times, working the dog on both sides. The handler should now start to vary where he stands in relationship to the dog so that eventually it is possible to stop the dog on the contact regardless of where the handler is positioned.

Once the dog is reliable, slowly raise the A-frame until the dog is doing full height.

If Your A-Frame Can't Be Lowered
If you are unable to lower the A-frame, complete Stages 1 through 3 of the training on the dog walk and Stages 1 and 2 of the see-saw training before trying the A-frame. Then work the A-frame as previously described.

Figure 2-13
All four feet should be on the contact.

Figure 2-14
Place the dog just above the contact.

Figure 2-15
The dog must wait on the contact until released.

The Dog Walk: Method 2 for Experienced Handlers

You can teach this method on a regulation height dog walk. However, if your dog walk is adjustable, lower it for Stages 3 through 5.

Stage 1

Decide which side of the obstacle is to be the down contact. With the dog facing away from the obstacle, have the handler lift him up and place him, with all four feet, on this contact, giving his contact command as he does so. The handler should hold the dog here and praise lavishly, giving a tidbit if he wishes. The handler should *not* use a WAIT command—the dog must learn to stop on the contact himself. After several seconds, have the handler give the release word and walk the dog off the obstacle.

Repeat this at least ten times during each training session, remembering to have the dog both on the right side as well as the left as the handler lifts the dog onto the obstacle.

Only move on to Stage 2 when the dog will wait on the contact without being held. This may take several training sessions.

Stage 2

With the dog on the lead, have the handler pick him up and place him just above the down contact. Giving his contact command, the handler should walk the dog onto the contact and then praise and continue on as in Stage 1. Repeat this many times, working the dog on both sides.

Repeat Stage 2, working the dog *off the lead*. Only move on to Stage 3 when the dog is reliable on Stage 2.

Stage 3

Before beginning this stage, lower the dog walk if possible. With the dog on the lead, have the handler lift him and place halfway down the down plank. The handler then quietly walks the dog down, giving his contact command as the dog reaches the contact. The handler should remember to praise and release as before.

Repeat many times, working the dog on both sides.

Slowly increase the distance the dog has to walk until he is doing Stage 3 from the top of the down plank.

Once the dog is reliable on the lead, try this stage *without the lead*. Only move onto Stage 4 when the dog is happily walking the down plank and stopping on the contact until released.

Stage 4

With the lead back on, have the handler lift the dog onto the centre of the top plank. The handler should then walk the dog along the plank to the down contact, giving his command for the contact just before the dog reaches it. The dog should stop on the contact until praised and released. If he doesn't, have the handler lift him back on and then repeat Stage 3 several times before coming back to Stage 4 again.

Repeat Stage 4 many times, working the dog both sides and slowly increasing the distance he walks until he is doing the entire top plank.

Repeat Stage 4 with the dog *off the lead*. Do not move on to Stage 5 until the dog is reliably doing Stage 4.

Stage 5

With the lead back on, have the handler quietly walk the dog over the whole obstacle. The handler should give the command for the contact just before the dog reaches it, and keep him on the contact for a few seconds before praising and releasing.

Repeat many times, working the dog on both sides.

Once the dog is happy doing this, repeat Stage 5 *without the lead*.

Slowly raise the height of the dog walk until the dog is doing it at full height. At this stage the handler should begin to vary his position in relationship to the contact. Sometimes stand behind the dog, sometimes in front. Also move out to the side at times.

The Cross-Over: Method 2 for Experienced Handlers

If you have access to this obstacle, contact training can be carried out on this as well. The progression of the stages would be the same as for the dog walk, Stage 4 being done from the table top.

The See-Saw: Method 2 for Experienced Handlers

This training is done with a regulation see-saw.

Stage 1

Using the plank on the ground as the down contact (the normal up plank), have the handler lift the dog up and place him, with all four feet, on this contact, giving his contact command as he does so. The handler should hold the dog here and praise lavishly, giving a tidbit if he wishes. The handler should *not* use a WAIT command—the dog must learn to stop on the contact himself. After several seconds, have the handler give the release word and walk the dog off the obstacle.

Repeat this at least ten times during each training session, remembering to have the dog both on the right as well as the left as you lift him onto the obstacle.

Only move onto Stage 2 when the dog will wait on the contact without being held. This may take several training sessions.

Stage 2

With the dog on the lead, have the handler pick him up and place him just the down contact (still using the "wrong" end of the see-saw as the down contact). Giving his contact command, the handler should walk the dog onto the contact, praise and continue on as in Stage 1.

Repeat many times, working the dog on both sides.

Once the dog is reliable on the lead, try this stage without the lead.

Figure 2-16
Using the side on the ground as the down contact, lift the dog onto the plank.

Slowly increase the distance the dog walks until he is being placed just before the point where the plank would move.

Stage 3

Before starting this stage, let the dog see and hear the plank move. Position an assistant behind the handler. Holding the dog by the collar, the handler walks the dog quietly up the plank and stops him at the tip point using a WAIT command. The handler holds the dog here while the assistant smoothly and slowly tips the plank. Once the plank is on the ground, walk the dog down as in Stage 2.

Repeat several times working the dog on both sides.

Stage 4

With the lead on, have the handler quietly walk the dog up the plank, giving a WAIT command at the tip point. The handler should help the plank down, until the dog has learned how to control it himself, and then walk the dog onto the contact, giving the contact command just before the dog reaches it. Be sure that the handler keeps the dog on the contact for a few seconds before praising and releasing.

Repeat many times working the dog on both sides.

When the dog is ready, repeat Stage 4 working without the lead. If at any time the dog does not stop on the contact until released, the handler should place his foot on the plank to hold it down and lift the dog back on.

Getting Ready for Competition

When the dog is reliably doing all of the contact obstacles with a good stop on the down contact, the handler can begin to release the dog sooner. Once competing, the release will come almost instantly when the dog reaches the contact. In training I advise the handler to always keep the dog on the contact for a few seconds before releasing. In competition, if the dog has already made a mistake, it is a good idea to keep him on the contacts for a few seconds before releasing. In this way, you can reinforce your training and hopefully prevent contact problems arising.

Unfortunately, even Method 2 is not foolproof and problems can arise, but dogs trained in this way do seem to focus their attention on the down contact and thus are much more reliable than those taught by Method 1. However, for it to be successful it is vital to work through all the stages.

Figure 2-17
Now place the dog above the contact.

Figure 2-18
Give a WAIT command at the tip point and then help the plank down.

Chapter Three The Weave Poles

Chapter Three
The Weave Poles

This, one of the hardest obstacles to teach the dog, is also the obstacle that more classes are won or lost over. A dog that weaves slowly can waste many vital seconds. A fast weaving dog is one that really enjoys this obstacle.

So how do you go about ensuring that a dog enjoys weaving? I think that initial training is very important.

Weave Pole Training Methods

There are several different ways to teach the weave poles.

- **The Push and Pull Method.** This is the method that most people used in the early days of Agility. The poles used are standard weave poles and the dog is persuaded to go through them, usually on the lead, encouragement being given by the use of a tidbit or a toy. Dogs taught in this way learn the accuracy first. Hopefully, the speed will follow later.

- **The "Weave-A-Matic".** This method uses poles with the bases in line that are angled out to each side so that the dog runs straight through without bending at all at first. As the dog progresses, the poles are slowly brought up to the vertical position and the dog learns to bend through them.

- **The Parallel Poles.** Sometimes called the "cage" or the "chute", two parallel rows of poles are set widely apart at first. Wires on each row keep the dog in the poles as he runs through. The poles are slowly moved together as the dog progresses until he is weaving correctly.

Both of the latter two methods teach the speed first, and accuracy follows later. Of these two methods I much prefer the parallel poles for several reasons:

- The movement used by the dog is similar to the final movement used when a dog weaves correctly.

- The wires prevent the dog from running out at the sides.

- The handler can easily work the dog on both sides right from the start.

Commands

The most common commands for this obstacle are WEAVE and POLES. I prefer WEAVE as I find it easier to get excitement in the voice with this command. I don't like two word commands, such as IN and OUT, as I always feel that the handler could confuse the dog by giving the command in the wrong place.

Figure 3-1
The Weave-
A-Matic

Figure 3-2
The cage or
chute.

Teaching the Weave Poles

This then is the method I use to teach weaving.

Equipment

Set up two parallel lines of weave poles as shown in Figure 3-3.

As with standard weave poles it is important that the dog always enters with the first pole on his left, so make sure that the left row is ahead of the right row. It is also important to use an equal number of poles so that the dog can enter correctly from both ends. Wires connect the poles in each line.

Training Notes

• Repetition and excitement are vital in the teaching of weaving. I find that using the words "Ready, Steady, Go!" is very good for getting the dog really keen before he is released. Ideally, weave poles need to be practised at least once a day. Several short sessions are much better than one long one. Handlers should be encouraged to set up some training weaves at home so that they can practise

Figure 3-3
Parallel poles set up for training.

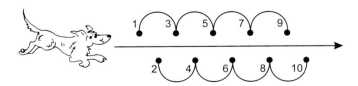

• Never be in a hurry to rush on to the next stage. The dog needs to be happily running through the poles with the handler on either side, going ahead of the dog on occasions and also staying at the start sometimes. If the dog has learned to jump, a low hurdle can be done before and after the poles. Remember the praise and a game each time.

Stage 1

Set the two lines of poles 18 inches to 24 inches apart, depending on the size of the dog.

The first time the dog does the poles, I always get the handler to walk through with the dog on leash. This gives the dog a chance to see and smell these strange things he is being asked to walk through. The handler may find it easier to walk backwards.

With the teaching of weaving it is vital to give the dog some incentive to go to. The first incentive I use is the handler himself. Starting with the dog just in the poles, I hold him while the handler walks through the poles to the other end. Once out of the poles, the handler turns and calls the dog using the WEAVE command as well as COME. Give lots of praise and repeat several times. The handler walking through the poles for these first few attempts means that he leaves a scent trail for the dog to follow and the dog will be less likely to jump out at the side.

Figure 3-4
The handler walks through the poles, turns around, and calls the dog.

Stage 2

Using a tidbit or a toy as the incentive, the handler is now going to begin to send the dog through the poles. I prefer a toy to a tidbit as I always find tidbits encourage the dog to sniff around. However, some dogs are only motivated by food so that sometimes you may have to use a tidbit.

Start the dog just in the poles, either making him wait or having an assistant hold him. The handler goes and places the toy about a foot away from the end of the poles. Then returning to the dog, the handler gets him really excited before sending him with a WEAVE command through the poles to the toy. The handler then runs past the poles to the dog and they have a game.

Repeat this several times with the handler running on both sides of the poles.

As the dog progresses he can be started further back so that he now enters the poles himself. Also, once the dog really understands that he has to go through the poles, the handler can begin to throw the toy. Now it won't matter if it lands a little to one side as the dog will not be so likely to jump out. The handler can even try staying at the start and recalling the dog back through the poles at times.

Figure 3-5
Get the dog really excited before letting him go.

Figure 3-6
A send-away and then a recall through the poles.

Stage 3

During this phase of training, the poles are gradually moved closer together until the dog is knocking against them as he runs through. He is still not bending, but he will feel the poles against his sides. At first the poles can be moved closer together about 1 inch at a time and the dog will not notice the difference. After each move, the poles should be left at this distance for *at least* a week. Once the poles are close enough for the dog to knock against, it will become necessary to stake the bases so that the dog does not push them apart as he goes through.

If at any time the dog should start to jump out of the chute, move the poles apart slightly and give more practise before trying them closer again.

Once the dog is knocking against the poles, it is important to take the time to get him really happy and confident before moving on to the next stage.

Stage 4

During this phase of training, the poles are very slowly moved closer together and the dog begins to bend through them. Move the poles no more than one-half inch at first, and even less as the poles get closer together.

If problems occur, never be afraid to move the poles apart slightly and give the dog further practise. This is the time when many handlers get impatient and want to rush. But lots of repetition is needed before the poles are finally in line and the dog is weaving correctly with the help of the wires. I then usually keep the dog at this stage for at least a month before moving to Stage 5.

Stage 5

This is the stage where the wires are removed and the dog finally comes to do a standard set of weave poles. Before starting to remove the wires, I always move the two lines of poles 1 inch apart. This makes the final stage much easier.

Figure 3-7
A lot of repetition is necessary at this stage of training.

Figure 3-8
The handler works the side without the wires.

There are two ways that the wires can be removed:

• If each wire is separate, the centre wires can be removed on both sides. The wires at the beginning and end are left to assist entry and exit. Remove the wires one at a time and get the dog really happy with each change before moving on. Finally, remove these last two wires and get the dog happy without wires before moving the lines of poles very slowly back together.

• The second way to remove the wires (and the only way if each line of poles is wired together) is to remove the wires completely on one side. The handler should then place himself on the side of the dog away from the poles as shown in Figure 3-8 so that he is using his body to keep the dog in the poles. By working from both ends, the handler can still practise the poles on either side. Once the dog is happy with this, the second row of wires can be removed. If the wires can be removed separately, remove the end one first and work back until the first wire is finally removed. If the poles and wires are not separate, I still remove them one at a time, standing the removed poles out to the side and replacing them with ordinary poles. Get the dog happy without wires before moving the lines of poles *very* slowly back together.

Once the poles are back in line and the dog is weaving happily, it is time to move to the final stage of training.

Stage 6

The focus here is getting the dog used to doing different weave poles. This is the stage where I find that with most dogs you get a slight "hiccup" in training. With every dog that I have trained in this way, I have gotten through the first five stages fairly easily, until the dogs were weaving well through standard poles placed in the bases of the training weaves. However, move these same poles into different bases (even with putting the new bases in exactly the same spot as the training ones were previously), and the reaction of all dogs when asked to weave is "Help Mum, what is this strange obstacle you are asking me to do?" The only reason for this behaviour that I can think of, is the smell of the bases.

I don't worry about this problem now. I simply go back to the old push and pull method for a few days. Use a toy and keep it as much fun as possible. So far I have found that in just a few days the penny seems to suddenly drop and it becomes "Hey Mum, why didn't you tell me these are the same—look I can weave!" You do lose the speed for a while but it very quickly comes back once the penny has dropped and I have found that other different looking poles rarely cause problems. Thus, even with this slight hitch I would always train my dogs in this method and advise others to use it.

Figure 3-9
Use a toy and keep it fun until the speed comes back.

A Variation on the Push and Pull Method

I sometimes have beginners come who are not prepared to put a lot of work into teaching the dog to weave. In this case, they are better sticking to ordinary poles and the old method. I find this is made much easier for the dog by using poles that stick in the ground and setting them up as follows:

1. Place six or eight poles in a straight line about 2 feet apart. It is important to use an even number of poles.

2. Move the second, fourth, sixth, and eighth pole out about 3 inches to the right. Staggering the poles just this little bit makes it easier for the dog because he doesn't have to bend so much.

The handler uses a toy or tidbit to encourage the dog to go through the poles. If the poles used are only about 2 feet high, the handler will be able to guide the dog through on the lead.

As the dog progresses, the poles are slowly moved closer until the dog is doing the weave poles in line.

Figure 3-11
If shorter poles are used, the handler can guide the dog through on lead.

Once the Dog Can Weave

Whichever method is used to teach the dog to weave, his training on this obstacle still has a long way to go even after he has learned how to negotiate standard poles.

He will need a lot of practise before he is reliable at:

• Entering ahead of his handler.

• Entering from all different angles.

• Weaving well regardless of handler position.

Chapter Four Tunnels, Tyre and Table

Chapter Four
Tunnels, Tyre and Table

In this chapter I will cover my methods for teaching tunnels, the tyre, and the table.

Tunnels

There are two types of tunnels used in Agility:

- The flat or collapsed tunnel

- The open or pipe tunnel (used in different shapes)

Which tunnel you introduce first is a matter of personal preference. Many people figure that the pipe tunnel is easier and do that first. I begin with the collapsed tunnel as I find that once the dog is happy going through that, the pipe tunnel presents no problem. Whereas, when introducing the pipe tunnel first, I find that most dogs balk for a time before doing it and then still have problems when first asked to go through a collapsed tunnel. I find doing the collapsed tunnel first cuts down the problems overall. I would prefer to have just one battle instead of two.

Commands

The most common commands are TUNNEL and THROUGH (as well as CHUTE in the U.S.). Tunnels and tyres are often close together on a course so don't use THROUGH for both.

Some handlers use a different command for each type. I use only one command. On the rare occasion a collapsed tunnel and pipe tunnel are side by side, I use direction commands to indicate the correct tunnel. This is the same way I tell the dog which end of a "C" shaped pipe tunnel I want him to go in.

Teaching the Collapsed Tunnel

This then is the method I use to teach the collapsed tunnel.

Stage 1

To introduce a dog to the collapsed tunnel, I hold him at the entrance while the handler goes to the other end, holds up the end of the chute, and crouches down. When the handler can *see* the dog, he calls him. I then "post" the dog into the tunnel and prevent him from coming back out by blocking the entrance with my body. I find that this works very well with the majority of dogs. Having a stranger hold the dog gives the dog more incentive to go through the tunnel to his handler. And, if the instructor is "posting" the dog into the tunnel, the dog is a lot less likely to struggle free and slip around the side of the tunnel.

Most dogs will struggle for a moment. I must stress that the dog is *NOT* forced into the tunnel. Rather, the dog is held in the entrance and prevented from coming out until he stops struggling and decides to go through to his handler who will then give *lots* of praise.

Repeat this until the dog is happily going through the tunnel to his handler. Most dogs are quite happy after two or three tries.

With a very nervous dog that is liable to panic if held by a stranger, it may be necessary to get the handler to bring someone the dog knows to hold him. Alternatively the handler can go into the tunnel with the dog. In this case it will be necessary to have the tunnel held open by an assistant.

Figure 4-1
"Posting" the dog through the tunnel to his handler.

Figure 4-2
An assistant is ready to stop the dog from coming back out.

Stage 2

Repeat Stage 1 but now as soon as the dog is in the tunnel, the handler should drop the chute so that the dog has to push through. An assistant ensures that the dog cannot come back out of the entrance and the handler gives lots of encouragement and praise.

Repeat several times, dropping the chute earlier each time, until the dog is happily pushing through without any help.

Stage 3

The handler now puts the dog into the tunnel before running to the end to call him. An assistant is ready to stop the dog from coming back out the entrance, if necessary. The handler should not call the dog until he is right at the end of the tunnel; calling the dog while the handler is still near the entrance will only encourage the dog to turn around. If the dog stops in the tunnel, the handler should be ready to lift up the end of the chute and call him again.

Repeat several times, working the dog on both sides.

Once the dog is happily going through the collapsed tunnel he can try the pipe tunnel.

Teaching the Pipe Tunnel

Once the dog is happily going through the collapsed tunnel, you can introduce him to the pipe tunnel.

Stage 1

Start with the pipe tunnel straight and fully extended. As with the collapsed tunnel, an assistant holds the dog at the entrance while the handler goes to the end and calls the dog. The handler should give lots of praise. The assistant should be ready to prevent the dog from coming back out by blocking the entrance with his body, if necessary.

Repeat several times.

Stage 2

The handler now puts the dog into the tunnel before running to the end to call him. An assistant is ready to prevent the dog from coming back out the entrance.

Repeat several times, working the dog on both sides.

Stage 3

As the dog progresses, the handler can begin to send him ahead into the tunnel.

Remember to work both sides.

Figure 4-3
The handler calls the dog through the pipe tunnel.

Figure 4-4
The pipe tunnel bent in a "C" shape.

Stage 4

Once the dog is happily going through a straight pipe tunnel, bend the tunnel into a gentle "C" shape and try that. At first it will probably be necessary for an assistant to block the entrance after the dog. When the dog can't see straight through the tunnel, he will be more likely to turn around.

Work the "C" shaped tunnel from left to right and from right to left.

Stage 5

When the dog is confident with the "C" shape, introduce an "S" shape and a tighter "C" shape.

The Tyre

Although there is only one type of tyre jump used in the U.S., there are several different designs used in Agility in the U.K.:

• *A rigid or fixed tyre.* This is a tyre which is fixed in a frame so that the tyre does not move at all.

• *A suspended tyre.* This is a type that's suspended in a frame and can move independently. There is usually a very inviting gap under the tyre and also gaps at the side. The dog has to learn that he must always jump though the tyre. The suspended tyre is the only type of tyre jump used in the U.S.

• *A lollipop tyre.* This tyre is stuck on a single pole with a foot that is staked to the ground for safety.

(Far left) Figure 4-5
A rigid tyre.
Photo by Russell Fine Art

(Center left) Figure 4-6
A suspended tyre.
Photo by Susan Morse

(Near left) Figure 4-7
A lollipop tyre.
Photo by Russell Fine Art

Figure 4-8
The handler calls the dog through the mini tyre, using a toy to help encourage him.
Photo by Russell Fine Art

Figure 4-9
The handler encourages the dog to jump through the tyre using a toy.
Photo by Russell Fine Art

Equipment

I introduce the dog to this obstacle using a low tyre. With big dogs I use my mini tyre (20 inches high at the centre of the aperture), and with mini dogs I use a tyre fixed on the ground. At first, a rigid tyre is better than a suspended one. The movement of a suspended tyre can bother some dogs when they are learning the obstacle.

Training Notes

• I think that the tyre is potentially the most dangerous obstacle on an Agility course. Care should always be taken to ensure that the dog jumps through straight and cleanly. A dog that jumps at an angle is at risk of banging his back. Although a dog "banking" or pushing off the inside of the tyre does not incur faults, he is much more likely to bang himself than a dog who jumps cleanly through the hole.

• Because a dog gets used to judging the height of the hole he is to jump through, I never like to vary the height of a tyre once the dog is jumping it at full height.

Commands

The most common commands are TYRE and HOOP (and THROUGH, if not used for tunnels).

Stage 1

An assistant holds the dog close up to the tyre. From the other side of the tyre, the handler shows the dog the hole and encourages him to jump through. The handler can use a toy to help entice the dog through the tyre. At first it may help to use a jump command as well as the tyre command.
Repeat several times.

Stage 2

The handler now encourages the dog to jump through the tyre without help from an assistant. If working on the lead, this should be passed through the tyre *before* the dog is asked to jump. The handler should give lots of praise.

Repeat several times working the dog on both sides.

Stage 3

As the dog progresses and is jumping higher, the height of the tyre can *slowly* be raised. If the dog suddenly loses confidence, you have probably raised the height too quickly and the tyre should be lowered again. If the dog will have to jump a 30 inch tyre in competition, I will make sure that he is happy jumping 24 inches before I put the tyre up to full height.

Stage 4

Once the dog is happy jumping a rigid tyre, he can be introduced to a suspended one.

Figure 4-10
First get a
fast down on
the ground.

Figure 4-11
Have the handler run with the dog and then down the dog in the pause box.

The Table

This is an obstacle that is often neglected in training. Because Agility trials in the U.K. are so big, there is rarely a table in standard classes. However, if you are lucky enough to qualify for a major finals, there is nearly always a table. Therefore, it is important to practise this obstacle. The table is also often used for the start and finish in a Gamblers class. In the U.S., the table is almost always used, although some organizations may require a sit on the table as well as a down. In other countries, the dog may also be asked to perform a stand on the table.

Equipment

In the beginning stages I use a pause box. However, a square marked out on the ground with jump poles or a suitable alternative will do just as well. I also use my mini table (15 inches high) in addition to the standard size table.

Commands

With this obstacle you need several commands. First, you need a command to tell the dog to get on the table—TABLE and BENCH are the most common. At first a jump command may help. But as soon as possible you want to drop this because jumps can be very close to the table in competition.

You also need a command to make the dog lie down—usually DOWN or FLAT (and a command for SIT and STAND, if you will be required to put the dog in these positions on the table). If on receiving this command a dog jumps back off the table, check what command the handler uses at home to get the dog off the furniture. Very often this is the same command so that the dog is only obeying his handler when he jumps off the table.

Figure 4-12
Now get a down on the mini table.

Finally, you need a command to make the dog wait on the table—normally WAIT or STAY.

Stage 1
First I make sure that the handler can make the dog go down quickly on the ground. If not, they must practise this skill until the dog will go down quickly on command.

Stage 2
Using a pause box (a square marked out on the ground with jump poles will do just as well), I have the handler run up to the box with the dog on the left, down the dog in the box, and make him wait for a few seconds.

Repeat this working the dog on the right.

Stage 3
Repeat Stage 2 now working with the mini table (15 inches high). When the dog first jumps on the table the handler should be sure to give lots of praise. Make sure the dog is happy on the table before the handler asks him to lie down. If the dog is unsure, put him in a sit rather than a down until he is happier on the table.

Stage 4
Once the dog is happily going down on the mini table, use this as a stepping stone to the big table.

Practise leaving the dog in the down while the handler walks over to another piece of equipment. You can save yourself time and running if you can do this in competition.

Stage 5
Finally when the dog is jumping higher hurdles he should be ready to do the full size table without the stepping stone.

Figure 4-13
The mini table is a stepping stone.
Photo by Russell Fine Art

Chapter Five Early Direction Control Training

Chapter Five
Early Direction Control Training

Once the dog can do the different obstacles he needs to learn to string these obstacles together so that eventually the handler can run a full course at speed with the dog under complete control. Being able to turn the dog in all directions and keep his attention when passing obstacles are skills that the handler needs to be successful. Let's have a look at how the handler can control the dog in Agility.

Direction Commands

There are three direction commands to teach the dog—a command to turn to the right, one to turn left, and one to go straight ahead. A fourth command which can be classed as a direction command is the command to COME.

There are two different ways of using direction commands. The way I use them is to turn the dog. These commands are not based on my position. For example, if the dog is coming towards me and I want to turn him to *MY* right, I have to give him a command to turn LEFT.

Direction commands are also used in relationship to the handler's position so that you have a command that turns the dog away from you and a command that turns him towards you. Lots of handlers use this method successfully, but I find that with a very fast dog it is difficult for the handler to be in the right position to use commands in this way.

Voice Commands

Voice commands need to be short and clear to the dog. Everything happens quickly in Agility and the dog must understand your command immediately. I find the first syllable of a command is the most important so don't use THIS WAY to turn right and THAT WAY to turn left. RIGHT and LEFT are good commands, but you can use whatever suits you as long as you don't confuse your dog.

Body Language

Body language can be used in several ways:

- *Hand signals.* These can be small movements of just the hand to show the dog the direction in which to move, or they can be movements of the whole arm. When using hand signals I find it best to use the hand nearest the dog; using the opposite one can attract the dog's attention across the handler's body and make him likely to run past obstacles.

- *Whole Body Movement.* Again this can be a small movement to one side or a complete change of direction by the handler.

- *Body and Dog Positioning.* An example of this is where the handler sets up the dog at the start line on his right when a sharp turn to the left comes early in the course.

Figure 5-1
*Usually it's best to use the
hand nearest the dog to signal.*

Most handlers use a combination of voice and body language. Whatever command you use, the most important thing is *timing*. Correct timing can make the difference between an average Agility performance and a super Agility performance. A command to turn given too early can turn the dog before the intended obstacle; a late command and the dog has either done the wrong obstacle or wasted time running on ahead. This timing is equally important when body language is used. Dogs see movement better than static things. The handler suddenly moving over is bound to attract his attention.

Teaching Direction Control

So you want to teach direction control. Do you use voice commands, body language, or a combination of both? Obviously, the decision is yours. Some handlers say they cannot think fast enough to use voice commands or they have difficulty telling right from left. These handlers will probably choose not to give voice directions to the dog but may use directions in relationship to themselves. As long as it works and both you and the dog are happy then fine, train in this way. However, if in the future you find that you are having problems with maybe a faster dog, never be afraid to try something else.

One of the common problems I see with handlers who rely on body movement alone is that the dog has to watch them and may not look where he is going. Also, a lot of hand signals can encourage a dog to jump up at the handler. Another problem is that sometimes the dog can misinterpret body language

when the handler is simply trying to move around a course. I find a combination of both voice commands and body language is best. Then if you do give the wrong voice command but your body language is right, the dog may still go the right way. Also, if direction commands have been taught well and you find yourself in the wrong place so that your body language is wrong, an emphasised voice command may save the day.

The way I introduce direction commands to a dog differs depending to a certain degree on the experience of the handler.

Teaching the Dog With an Experienced Handler

• *Heelwork.* I always begin each training session with a short warm-up exercise. This is designed to get the dog settled down, listening to his handler, and ready for work. Whenever possible this warm up is done around Agility obstacles, which gets the dog used to passing equipment without taking it. Direction commands can be given every time the handler turns. At first this will need to be done on lead. Later it should be done off lead. When passing equipment off lead, I always feel it is better to emphasise the HEEL or direction command turning away from equipment than to keep saying "No!" to stop the dog from performing the obstacle. I get handlers to do this heelwork with their dog on both the left and the right. The COME command can also be practised by the handler occasionally backing away from the dog and calling him.

• *Jumping Exercises.* With a dog new to Agility it is very important that you get good forward movement before teaching sharp turns. So jumping exercises for the first few weeks will be limited to straight lines and large circles. However, even with a straight row of jumps you can start to teach the turn commands. At the end of the straight line of jumps when the dog is on your left, you give a command RIGHT, turn that way, and run on a few yards before praising the dog. When the dog is on your right, you obviously command and turn LEFT.

The Dog with an Inexperienced Handler

With an inexperienced handler I still use the above exercises but I take it slowly so that the handler does not get confused. With this in mind, in early lessons I only work on one turn command at a time.

Teaching the Send-Away

Being able to send on and work your dog ahead of you is a very useful accomplishment for an Agility handler. You save yourself a lot of running and can save a lot of time if you are able to send the dog on ahead. No handler can run as fast as their dog so that if he will not go on well, the dog has to wait for the handler to catch up. Being able to work your dog at a distance is also very necessary if you want to do well in Gamblers classes.

So how do you start to teach these skills to the dog? I find the earlier you start the better so that my beginner dogs will do a lot of work on send-aways. See the lessons in Chapter 7 and also in Volume III.

Chapter Six Organizing Beginner Agility Classes

Chapter Six
Organizing Beginner Agility Classes

When a new handler and dog turns up ready to start Agility training, there are several things that a good instructor checks before allowing the handler to join a class.

Age of the Dog

Repeated jumping and pulling himself over the A-frame can place a strain on a dog's legs and shoulders. Therefore, the dog's bones need to be mature before he starts. This will vary from breed to breed with the larger, heavy-boned breeds taking longer to mature. As a general rule, I like all dogs to be at least twelve months old before they start regular Agility training*, and the larger, heavy-boned dogs I like to be at least fifteen months old.

* I am not including puppy Agility training here; this is done younger and is covered in *Agillity Fun The Hobday Way, Volume I.*

Fitness of the Dog

A dog needs to be fit to do Agility. Obviously the dog will get fitter as his lessons progress, but there are things that need to be checked first. I always get the handler to trot the dog up and down. This can be done as a warm-up exercise. Watch to see if the dog moves freely and happily. If the dog shows any sign of distress, get the handler to have the dog checked over by a vet before he starts jumping.

I always like to have a word with each dog, and while doing so, I check to make sure that the dog is not overweight. It is unfair to ask an overweight dog to do much Agility. When I do find a fat dog, I tactfully suggest that a diet will help and I don't allow the dog to do more than very low jumps until he has lost weight.

Handler Control

Many clubs insist that handlers complete an Obedience course before they begin Agility classes. With the classes that I run, however, I do not require this. I find some handlers will be put off trying Agility if they are told that they must wait for several months. Also, if you insist on them reaching a certain standard of Obedience before allowing them to start Agility, some handlers may never make the grade. I find that a lot of Obedience is taught through Agility and handlers very soon realise that they are not going to get very far until they have control of their dog. In many ways I would rather have handlers who have not done a lot of Obedience. They don't have so many problems with working the dog on the right.

Although I don't insist that a handler has done Obedience training, he does need to be able to control his dog so that the dog is not a nuisance to other dogs in the class. If a dog is a nuisance to others, I get the handler to have some private training until the problem is sorted out. Then he can rejoin the class.

Equipment Necessary for the Dog

- *Collar.* When a dog competes in Agility he is not allowed to wear a collar. However, it is useful to have a collar on when training. This should be a plain leather or nylon collar, not a choke or check collar. This is for the dogs safety; even a half-check collar could get caught up on equipment and frighten, if not injure the dog. Also, having a loop hanging down is dangerous as the dog could catch a foot in it. With beginner dogs it is important for the instructor to check that the collar is fastened tightly enough. Avoidable problems can be caused by the collar pulling off over the dog's head.

- *Lead.* Although you should work towards removing the lead as soon as possible, it will be necessary to use it for a time with the majority of beginner dogs. The lead should be 3 to 4 feet long and made of leather, rope, or nylon. Chain leads should not be used as the chain can get caught up on obstacles and is hard on the handler's hands.

- *Training tab.* This is a very useful piece of equipment and often bridges the gap between working the dog on lead and off lead. It is easily made from an old lead with a usable clip. The lead should be cut about 6 to 10 inches away from the clip. The length depends on the size of the dog. The tab shouldn't be so long that the dog can step on it and trip himself. It is also important that the handler doesn't put a loop in the end as the dog could get a foot stuck in it.

Equipment Necessary for the Handler

- *Shoes.* The instructor should ensure that the handler knows what type of shoes is best for the surface involved. It can be very disconcerting for a new handler to be slipping and sliding in unsuitable shoes while trying to control his dog.

- *Clothes.* As well as suitable clothes if working outside, the handler should be encouraged to wear fairly tight fitting clothes. Anything that flaps around beside the dog's head will distract the dog and encourage him to jump up at his handler.

- *Toys.* I am a great believer in the use of toys for motivation in Agility. Many beginner handlers have to be told to find their dogs a toy and even shown how to teach their dogs to play. A good instructor will always have a selection of toys available if the handler forgets to bring one. In a class situation, toys that don't squeak or have lost their squeak are best. A squeaking toy in a class will distract a lot of dogs.

- *Tidbits.* Although I personally prefer toys, tidbits do have a place in Agility training. Used correctly, tidbits can be very useful. However, the tidbits used should be small enough to be eaten quickly and not leave a trail of crumbs to distract the next dog.

Introducing the Agility Obstacles

There are many ways of organising beginner Agility classes. One of the biggest problems with Agility classes is that all dogs progress differently and after just a couple of weeks with a class of beginners you will have a wide range of ability. The instructor needs to take this into account when planning lessons.

First, how do you organise the introduction to the obstacles?

On a One-to-One Basis

I find that a private lesson—one handler and dog with the full attention of the instructor—is one of the best ways to introduce a dog to the Agility equipment. The dog has fewer distractions and can progress at his own speed. A disadvantage of this method is that if the dog has a lot of problems, the handler may get disheartened and think that no one else has such problems. Also, it is very concentrated training for the dog that tires easily. As long as the instructor bears these two factors in mind, I find that this is an excellent way to introduce a dog to Agility.

When using this method it is important that the dog does not get tired or bored. I find that changing from one type of obstacle to another prevents this. Here is a quick run down of the order in which I introduce a new dog to the equipment. Spend no more than five to ten minutes on each item.

1. *Warm-up heelwork.* This gives me the chance to assess the handler's control and the dog's fitness. I can also see the handler's reaction to running the dog on the right.

2. *Jumps*

3. *A-frame*

4. *Collapsed or flat tunnel*

5. *Dog walk*

6. *Pipe tunnel*

7. *Weave poles.* This is mainly an explanation of how it's best to teach this obstacle. While this is happening, the dog is having a short rest.

8. *Tyre*

9. *Table*

10. *See-saw.* This is only done with dogs that are happy on the dog walk.

11. *Long jump*

12. Finally we put together the obstacles the dog can now do into a simple straight line course. This I find gives the handler a real sense of achievement.

I haven't gone into detail of how I introduce each obstacle as this is covered in Chapters 1 through 4.

This private lesson takes between an hour and an hour and a half. Some dogs will cover everything, some won't. Each dog progresses at *his own* rate. I find that the majority of handlers and dogs are able to fit into a beginner class after just one private lesson.

Within an Existing Class
One of the problems with trying to organise a beginner class can be the handler and dog who turns up a few weeks after the class has begun. Of course you can insist that they wait for the next beginner course, but if this is not starting for several weeks you may lose this particular handler's interest. One way around this problem is to have an assistant instructor who works with this new handler and introduces him to each piece of equipment while it is not being used in the main class.

A disadvantage here is that the new dog finds lots to look at and be distracted by. In addition, it may not be so easy to lower contact equipment when it is also being used by a class. However, at least you won't have lost a potential customer, and after a couple of weeks with a helper, the new handler may be able to join in the class properly.

Teaching the Beginner Class
A class is probably how most people get their introduction to Agility. How this class is organised and the quality of instruction is very important. Many a would-be Agility handler has been put off by the experiences they and their dog have had in the beginner class. The instructor of the beginner class has a very important job and a club's most experienced instructor should be the one to take this class. Unfortunately, a lot of clubs put their new instructors in charge of beginners and it

can be a daunting task. Problems keep cropping up that need sorting out sympathetically, and dogs and handlers can easily become bored. Many new handlers give up after the first few weeks. This is a great shame and with careful instruction can be avoided.

These are some of the factors a good beginner class instructor keeps in mind.

- *Good Preparation.* This is important with any class but it is vital with a beginner class. The instructor should plan the class so that he or she always knows what to do next. Try to vary the type of obstacle being worked with to prevent the dogs from getting bored.

- *Be Adaptable.* Although planning is vital, the instructor should not be too rigid and should always be ready to change plans if something unexpected crops up. It is pointless sticking to your plan if you suddenly find the planned work is proving too difficult or too easy for the students.

- *Be Constructive in Criticism and Praise Handlers.* People are just like children and dogs—they work much better when praised. Destructive criticism will simply demoralise handlers and may even cause them to give up Agility. When you do need to criticise handling, make it constructive and try later in the session to find something to praise.

- *Concentration Span.* When dogs first begin Agility their attention span will be very short, so keep exercises short and encourage handlers to give lots of praise and play. Remember, handlers can also suffer from lack of concentration and you may sometimes need to explain things several times.

- *Be in Control at All Times.* A good instructor knows what everyone in the class is doing. Beginner handlers must not be allowed to go off and do their own thing. This is when accidents can happen. An instructor must pleasantly insist on this rule.

- *Always Be Aware of Safety.* The dogs' safety should be top priority. Always ensure that waiting handlers and dogs are well out of the way of the working dog. Never over-face a dog by asking it to jump too high or tackle contact obstacles from funny angles. Beginner dogs should always approach obstacles straight on. They will learn awkward angles later.

- *Be Honest.* No one knows all the answers in Agility. So don't be afraid to admit you're wrong if something doesn't work. If you can't think of a solution to a problem, ask for suggestions from the class—they may surprise you. If necessary, tell the class you will think about the problem and try to find a solution by the next session. Every dog is different and we are learning all the time so don't try to make out you are a god. If you appear human, the class will respect you and work all the better. A good instructor is always approachable.

- *Keep It Fun.* Handlers and dogs will learn much quicker if they are enjoying themselves. A good instructor has a sense of humour and can use it when necessary. Agility should be fun for dog, handler *and* instructor.

Chapter Seven A Beginner Agility Class

Chapter Seven
A Beginner Agility Class

This chapter gives lesson plans for an eight-week beginner Agility class. The plans are designed for a class of ten to twelve dogs and handlers. I feel this is the largest number a single instructor should take.

Ideally with beginners, the instructor should have an assistant trainer who can help with any problems that crop up, help with dogs and handlers that miss a class, and supervise any practising of obstacles while the instructor is occupied elsewhere.

During this first eight-week course I shall gradually introduce all of the Agility obstacles so that by the last week the dogs have met all of the obstacles. With a smaller class it may be possible to introduce some obstacles sooner.

Working on the Lead

The majority of beginner Agility students may have to use the lead for the whole of this eight week class, and the work set out in this chapter is designed to be worked on the lead. However, a few handlers may be ready to work without the lead by Lesson 3 or 4. As having the dog on the lead restricts the dog's movement, it is important that the dog works free as soon as possible, and instructors should be happy to let handlers try without the lead as soon as they can.

Handlers who have completed a puppy Agility class may be able to work jumps without the lead from the start, although it probably will still be necessary to use the lead when first doing the contact obstacles.

Encourage handlers to try without the lead, but never be afraid to put it back on if necessary. A short training tab can be very helpful during the transition period.

Working the Dog on Both Sides

Working the dog on both the handler's left side *and* right side is desirable in Agility and taken into account in all of the exercises in this chapter. However, occasionally an instructor meets a dog that is very unhappy if asked to work on the handler's right. At this stage, it is more important to keep a dog happy with Agility than to force the dog to work both sides. Later when the dog is more confident, it may be possible to try again to get him working on both sides.

Raising the Height of Obstacles

The obstacles should be raised to regulation height very gradually over the duration of this eight-week class. It is always better to keep an obstacle low for longer than necessary than to over-face dogs.

With an average class I would expect all of the contact equipment to be at full height by Lesson 8, and the dogs happily jumping at least 6 inches lower than their final jump height.

The training weave poles should be moved slightly closer each week so that by Lesson 8 the dog is knocking against the poles but still not having to bend.

Warm-Up Exercises

I always begin each training session with a short warm-up exercise. This is designed to get the dog settled down, listening to his handler and so ready for work. Whenever possible this warm-up is done around Agility obstacles, which gets the dog used to passing equipment without taking it. At first this will need to be done on lead, later it should be done off lead.

When passing equipment off lead, I always feel it is better to emphasise the HEEL or direction command turning away from equipment than to keep saying "No!" to stop the dog from performing the obstacle.

I get handlers to do this heelwork with the dog on both the left and the right.

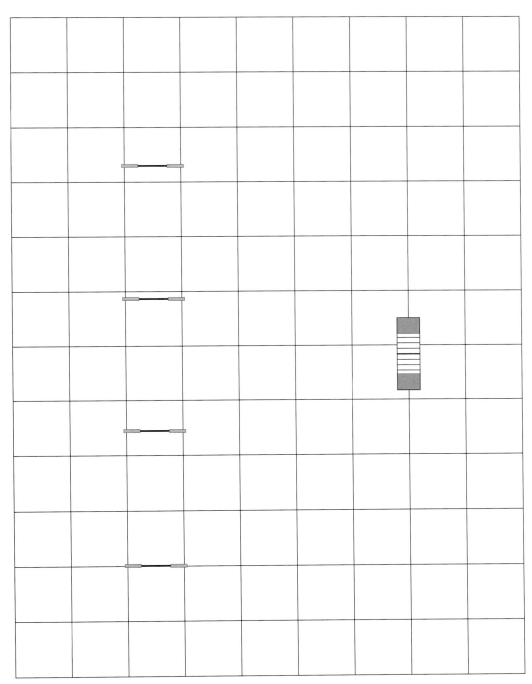

Equipment

- Four hurdles set in a straight line 8 paces apart with single poles set at 6 inches to 15 inches, depending on size of dog.

- A-frame set at its lowest height

Figure 7-1

LESSON 1 • *A Beginner Agility Class*

WORK TO DO	HINTS FOR INSTRUCTORS
Warm-up With the dog on the left, run at a steady trot in and out of the hurdles. Repeat working the dog on the right.	**Warm-up** Explain that in Agility the dog needs to look ahead rather than at the handler. Assess each handler's control over the dog. Note any handlers having difficulty.
Teaching the dog to jump With the dog on the left, both handler and dog go over the hurdles. Turn right after the last hurdle and walk back to the start. Give lots of praise. Repeat working the dog on the right. Repeat both of the previous steps. With the dog on the left, do the jumps with the handler running at the side, not over the jumps. Repeat working the dog on the right. Repeat both of the previous steps.	**Teaching the dog to jump** Discuss commands: JUMP, UP, OVER. If any handlers are happier with the dog on the right, let them work this side first. Any problems with the first hurdle should be sorted out before the dog does the whole row. If any dog is unhappy working on the right, let him stay on the handler's left for now. Some handlers and dogs may not need to repeat these exercises. Show handlers how to hold the lead to keep the dog in the centre of the jumps. Encourage handlers to give plenty of praise at the end of the line of jumps.

LESSON 1 • *A Beginner Agility Class*

WORK TO DO	HINTS FOR INSTRUCTORS
Introduce the A-frame With the dog on the left and holding the collar, walk the dog over the obstacle. Stop him on the down contact and praise. Repeat working the dog on the right. Repeat both of the previous steps. With the dog on the left, holding the lead, walk the dog over the obstacle. Stop him on the down contact and praise. Repeat working the dog on the right. Repeat both of the previous steps.	**Introduce the A-frame** Discuss commands: WALK ON, PLANK, CLIMB. Explain contact points and the importance of making the dog go to the bottom of the obstacle. The instructor should be on the opposite side of the handler, ready to assist if necessary. Make sure that the handler praises the dog on the down contact. Tell handler to be ready to stop the dog from jumping off at the side. If a dog does persist in jumping off the obstacle, put a lead on either side and use the leads to keep the dog in the centre of the A-frame.
Course Run the course shown in Figure 7-2 with the dog on the left and then repeat working the dog on the right.	**Course** Place a hurdle before and after the A-frame as illustrated in Figure 7-2. The instructor should be ready at the A-frame to help if necessary.

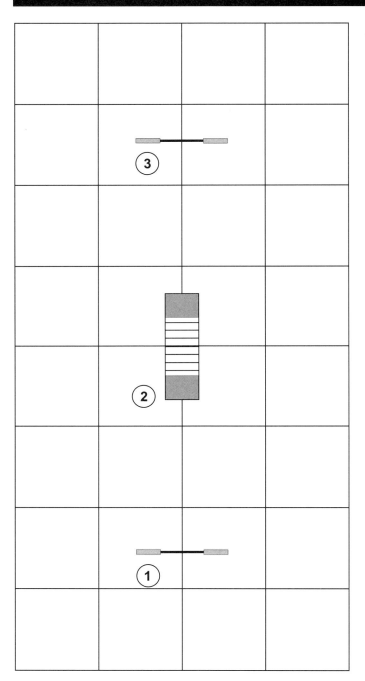

Figure 7-2

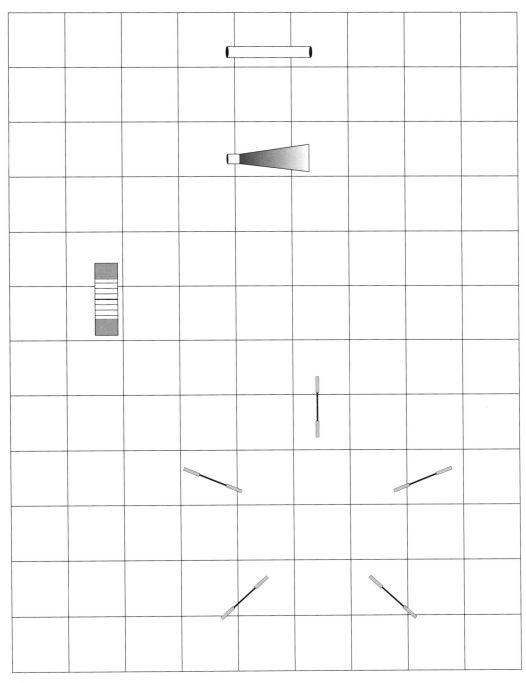

Figure 7-3

Equipment

- Five low hurdles set in a large circle with 7 to 8 paces between hurdles

- A-frame set low

- Collapsed tunnel

- Pipe tunnel

LESSON 2 • *A Beginner Agility Class*

WORK TO DO	HINTS FOR INSTRUCTORS
Warm-up With the dog on the left, run around the circle of jumps going in and out of jumps. Repeat working the dog on the right.	**Warm-up** Discuss commands: HEEL, CLOSE. Discuss commands: SIDE, BY ME.
Jumping With the dog on the left do the circle of jumps. Repeat working the dog on the right. Repeat the previous two steps.	**Jumping** Some handlers may need to go over the jumps with their dogs. Encourage a steady jog. Speed will come later. Remind handlers to praise their dogs.
Introduce the collapsed tunnel Have an assistant hold dog at the entrance. Handler holds up end of fabric and calls the dog through. Give lots of praise and encouragement. Repeat several times.	**Introduce the collapsed tunnel** Discuss commands: TUNNEL, THROUGH, CHUTE. Get the handler to start to drop the end of the fabric so that the dog has to push through. Block the entrance so that the dog cannot come back out.
Introduce the pipe tunnel Have an assistant hold dog at the entrance. Handler goes to other end and calls the dog through. Give lots of praise. Repeat several times.	**Introduce the pipe tunnel** To save time, have an assistant deal with the pipe tunnel. Send each handler to the pipe tunnel after his dog has done the collapsed tunnel.

LESSON 2 • *A Beginner Agility Class*

WORK TO DO	HINTS FOR INSTRUCTORS
A-frame Review the A-frame, working the dog on both sides. Repeat with the A-frame a little higher.	**A-frame** Check to make sure that handlers are stopping dogs on the down contact and praising. If dogs are ready, raise the obstacle a little.
Course Run the course shown in Figure 7-4 with the dog on the left and then repeat working the dog on the right.	**Course** Set up the course shown in Figure 7-4. Be ready to assist with the A-frame and block the tunnel entrance after the dog, if necessary.

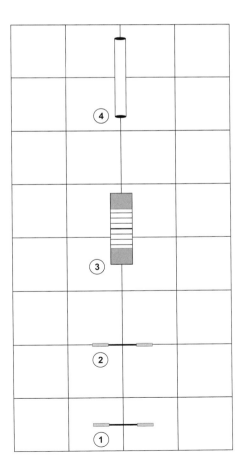

Figure 7-4

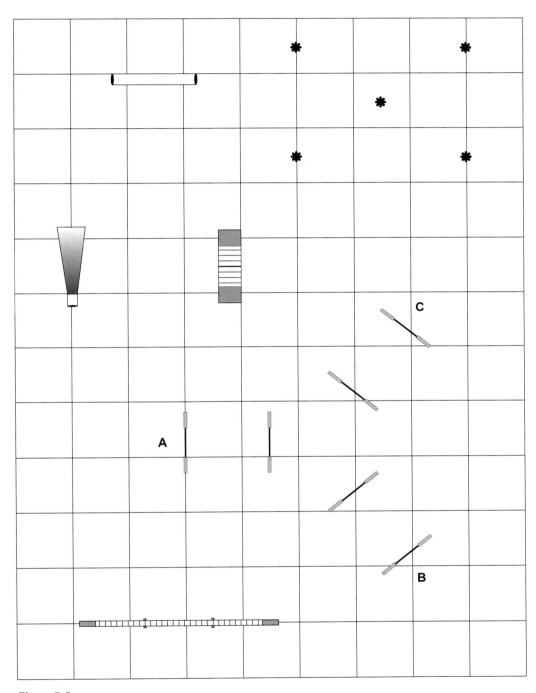

Equipment

- Five poles or cones set out as shown in Figure 7-5

- Six hurdles set as shown in Figure 7-5

- A-frame set low

- Pipe tunnel

- Collapsed tunnel

- Dog walk (lowered if it is possible)

Figure 7-5

WORK TO DO	HINTS FOR INSTRUCTORS
Warm-up With the dog on the left, start at pole 1, run to pole 2, turn right around pole 2, and then run back and go right around pole 1 as shown in Figure 7-6. Continue clockwise with the other poles (pole 3, then pole 4, then pole 5), doing pole 1 between each and turning right each time. Repeat working the dog on the right.	**Warm-up** Discuss commands for turning right: THIS WAY, RIGHT, CLOSE. Tell handlers to give the direction command just before the turn. The handler still turns the dog right.
Jumping With the dog on the handler's left, work the series of jumps from A to B. With the dog on the handler's right, work the series of jumps from A to C. With the dog on the handler's left, work the series of jumps from C to A. With the dog on the handler's right, work the series of jumps from B to A.	**Jumping** Handlers can give a turn command after jump #2 if they wish. However, at this stage it is more important to keep the flow going over the slight turn. Body language and the lead will help the dog do the correct jump.
Introduce the dog walk With the dog on the left and holding the collar, walk the dog over the obstacle. Stop him on the down contact and praise. Repeat working the dog on the right. Repeat both of the previous steps until the dog is going steadily over the obstacle. With the dog on the left, holding the lead, walk the dog over the obstacle. Stop him on the down contact and praise. Repeat working the dog on the right. Repeat both of the previous steps.	**Introduce the dog walk** Discuss commands: WALK ON, PLANK, CLIMB. Explain contact points and the importance of making the dog go to the bottom of the obstacle. The instructor should be on the opposite side to the handler, ready to assist if necessary. Make sure that the handler praises the dog on the down contact. Watch to make sure that the handler doesn't pull the dog off balance.

LESSON 3 • *A Beginner Agility Class*

WORK TO DO	HINTS FOR INSTRUCTORS
A-frame and tunnels Review these obstacles.	**A-frame and tunnels** If possible, have an assistant work with handlers on these obstacles.
Course Run the course shown in Figure 7-7 with the dog on the left. Repeat working the dog on the right.	**Course** Set up the course shown in Figure 7-7. Have an assistant at the collapsed tunnel entrance to hold dogs if necessary, and prevent them from coming back out. Turn the collapsed tunnel around.

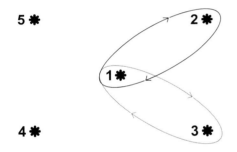

Figure 7-6

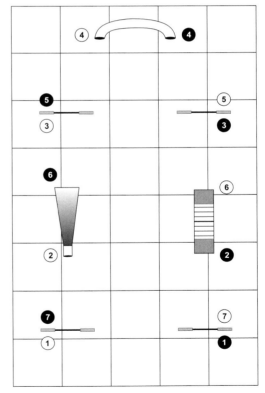

Figure 7-7

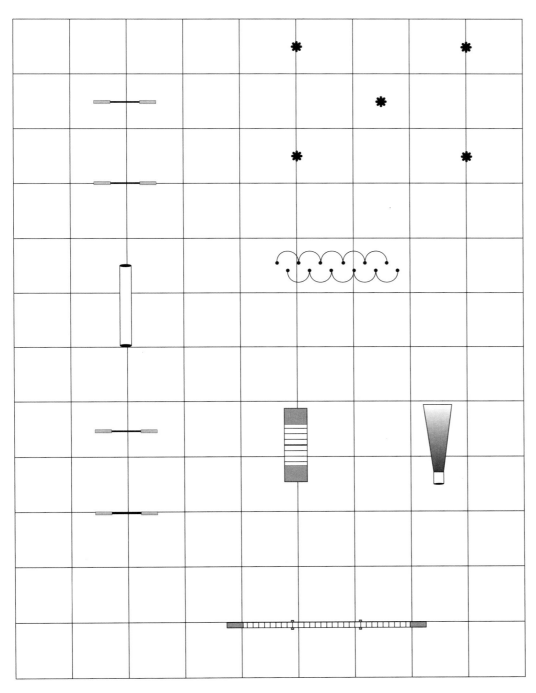

Equipment

- Five poles or cones set out as shown in Figure 7-8

- Two hurdles on each side of the pipe tunnel set out in straight line

- Dog walk, A-frame, and collapsed tunnel available for practise

- Training weave poles set 18 inches apart

Figure 7-8

LESSON 4 • *A Beginner Agility Class*

WORK TO DO	HINTS FOR INSTRUCTORS
Warm-up With the dog on the right, start at pole 1, run to pole 5, turn left around pole 5, and then run back and go left around pole 1 as shown in Figure 7-9. Continue counter-clockwise with the other poles (pole 4, then pole 3, then pole 2), doing pole 1 between each and turning left each time. Repeat working the dog on the left.	**Warm-up** Discuss commands for turning left: LEFT, BACK. Tell handlers to give the command just before the turn. The handler still turns the dog left.
Jumping With the dog on the left, do the row of jumps and the tunnel. Have a game with a toy at the end. Repeat working the dog on the right. Repeat the previous two steps several times.	**Jumping** Encourage handlers to try to get the dog looking ahead by throwing a toy over the last jump. Alternatively, position a "bait master" at the end of the row obstacles with a toy or tidbit as the bait. With dogs that are ready, slightly raise the jumps.
Introduce the weave poles An assistant holds the dog at the beginning of the poles while the handler walks through the poles and calls the dog. Give lots of praise. Repeat several times.	**Introduce the weave poles** Discuss commands: WEAVE, POLES. Demonstrate training methods and decide which handlers will use. Encourage handlers to use an excited voice.
A-frame, dog walk, and collapsed tunnel Review these obstacles several times, working the dog on both sides.	**A-frame, dog walk, and collapsed tunnel** If possible, have an assistant work with handlers on these three obstacles.
Course Walk the course shown in Figure 7-10 clockwise and then run it. Walk the course counter-clockwise and then run it.	**Course** Set up the course shown in Figure 7-10. Walk the course with the handlers, showing them how to line up their dogs for obstacles. Also discuss which side is best for handling the dog.

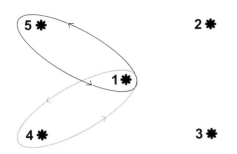

Figure 7-9

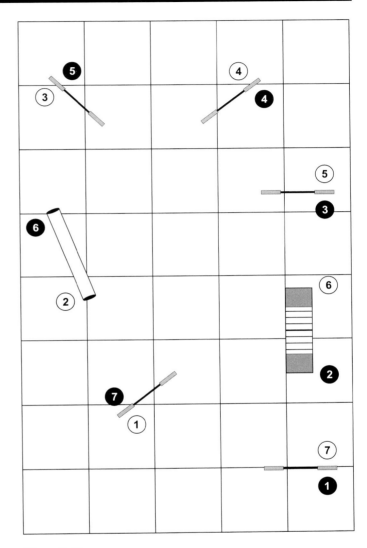

Figure 7-10

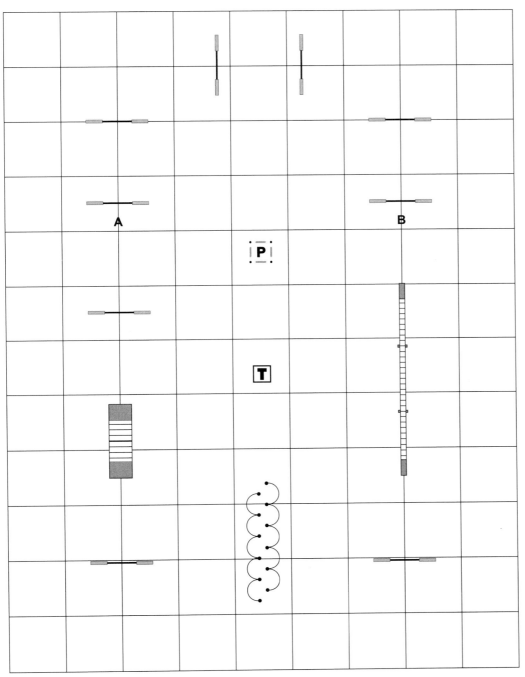

Equipment

- Six hurdles set out as shown in Figure 7-11

- Training weave poles available for practise

- Pause box

- Mini table (15 inches high)

- A-frame, dog walk, and three more hurdles set up in a course

Figure 7-11

WORK TO DO	HINTS FOR INSTRUCTORS
Warm-up With the dog on the left, run clockwise in and out of the six jumps shown at the top of Figure 7-11. Repeat running counter-clockwise with the dog on the right.	**Warm-up** Suggest that handlers give a command each time they turn right. Suggest that handlers give a command each time they turn left.
Jumping With the dog on the left, run the sequence of jumps shown in Figure 7-11 from A to B. Give a turn command after the second and fourth jumps. With the dog on the right, run from B to A. Repeat these two sequences several times.	**Jumping** Make sure handlers give RIGHT commands in the correct places. Suggest that handlers give a LEFT command. See if any dogs are ready to try the exercise off lead.
Training weave poles Starting with the dog on the left, send him through the weave poles to a toy or tidbit. Repeat several times. Repeat starting with the dog on the right.	**Training weave poles** Make sure that the toy or tidbit is placed in line with the poles and just beyond (about 2 feet) the exit of the poles. Make sure that the handler is using plenty of praise and keeping it a game.
Pause box With the dog on the left, run up to the pause box and down the dog. Wait a few seconds and then release the dog. Repeat working the dog on the right.	**Pause box** Discuss commands: BOX, DOWN, FLAT. The pause box can be baited with a toy or tidbit.
Introduce the table With the dog on the left, run up to the mini table and have him jump up onto it. Praise and play. Repeat working the dog on the right.	**Introduce the table** Discuss commands: TABLE, BENCH. At this stage get the dog happy jumping up onto the table. Bait the table with a toy or tidbit.

LESSON 5 • *A Beginner Agility Class*

WORK TO DO	HINTS FOR INSTRUCTORS
Flyball Teach the dog to catch a toy.	**Flyball** Check that toys are suitable.
Course Walk the course shown in Figure 7-12 clockwise and then run it. Walk the course counter-clockwise and then run it.	**Course** Have handlers run the course shown in Figure 7-12. Have an assistant by the A-frame and by the dog walk to help out dogs if necessary.

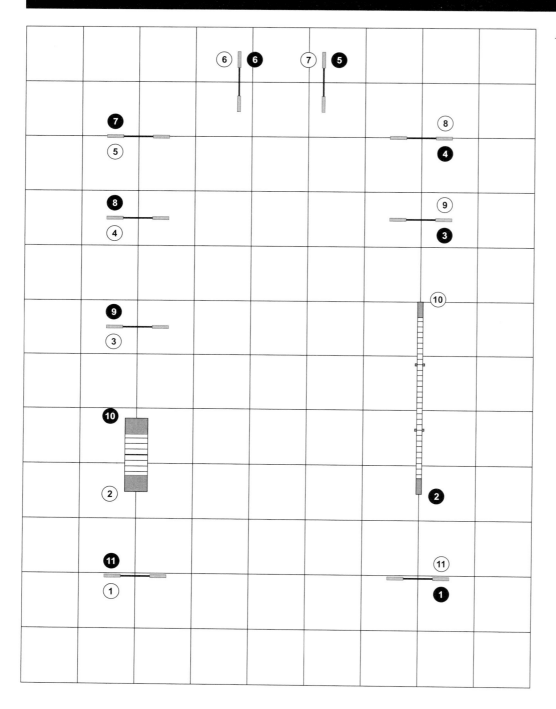

Figure 7-12

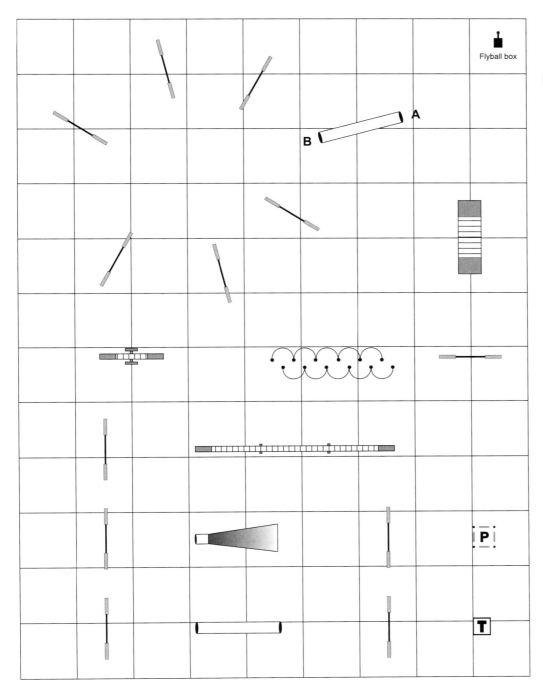

Flyball box

B **A**

Equipment

- Six hurdles and the pipe tunnel set out in a circle as shown in Figure 7-13

- Training weave poles available for practise

- Dog walk and A-frame each with a hurdle in front also available for practise

- See-saw

- Flyball box

- Collapsed tunnel, pipe tunnel, pause table, and pause box set up in a course with additional jumps

P

T

Figure 7-13

LESSON 6 • *A Beginner Agility Class*

WORK TO DO	HINTS FOR INSTRUCTORS
Warm-up Run in and out of the circle of jumps and past the pipe tunnel. Work the dog on both sides.	**Warm-up** Tell handlers to give a HEEL or SIDE command as they pass the tunnel rather than saying "No" to the dog.
Jumping An assistant holds the dog at A and the handler stands at B. The handler should call the dog through the tunnel and then do the circle of jumps clockwise with the dog on the left. Do the tunnel again. Repeat counter-clockwise with the dog on the right. Repeat the previous two steps.	**Jumping** Show handlers where to stand at B so that they are not in the dog's way and their body language is suggesting the way to turn. Let handlers work out where to stand now. Correct if necessary. If possible, make the dogs wait without being held.
A-frame and dog walk Practise doing the jump before each of these obstacles. Work the dog on both sides. Praise on the down contacts.	**A-frame and dog walk** Use an assistant for these obstacles. Check that dogs are going onto the obstacle straight and getting the contacts well.
Introduce the see-saw With the dog on the left and holding the collar, walk the dog up to the centre of the plank. Hold the dog there while an assistant lowers the plank. Walk the dog down, praising on the contact. Repeat twice with the dog on the right.	**Introduce the see-saw** Make sure that dogs are happy on the dog walk before allowing them to do the see-saw. Control the plank from behind the dog as this is less distracting. Only do the right when dogs are happy on the left.
Training weave poles Do several times working the dog on both sides.	**Training weave poles** If dogs are ready, move the poles slightly closer together.
Flyball box Try the flyball box.	**Flyball box** Explain the best way to teach this.

LESSON 6 • *A Beginner Agility Class*

WORK TO DO	HINTS FOR INSTRUCTORS
Send-away With the dog on the left, run the line of obstacles that ends with the pause box. Down and wait the dog in the box. Repeat working the dog on the right. Repeat the previous two steps. With the dog on the left, run the line of obstacles that ends with the table. Down and wait the dog on the table. Repeat working the dog on the right. Repeat the previous two steps.	**Send-away** Discuss the send-away command: AWAY, GO ON. The pause box can be baited with a toy or tidbit. Encourage handlers to begin to hang back. Bait the table with a toy or tidbit each time.

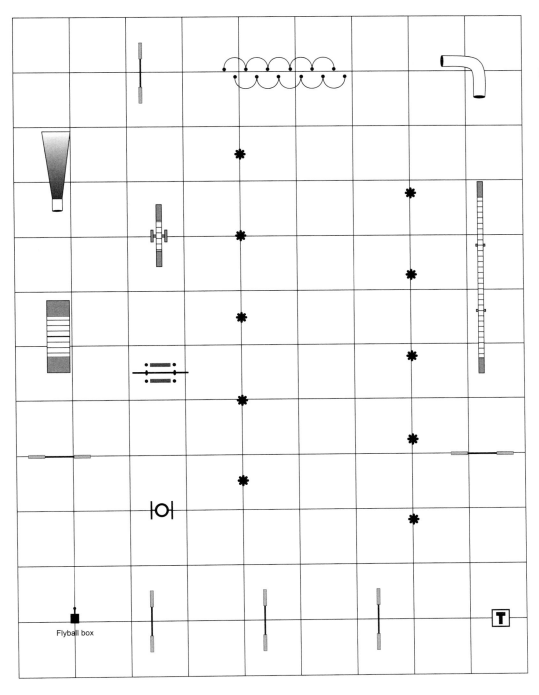

LESSON 7
A Beginner Agility Class

Equipment

- Ten poles or cones set out as shown in Figure 7-14

- Straight line of three hurdles to the mini table

- See-saw and flyball box available for practise

- Mini tyre

- Long jump set at 2'6" long with an 18" hurdle in the middle for big dogs or at 1'6" long with a 12" hurdle for mini dogs

- A-frame, collapsed-tunnel, pipe tunnel, dog walk, training weave poles, and three jumps set up in course

Flyball box

Figure 7-14

LESSON 7 • A Beginner Agility Class

WORK TO DO	HINTS FOR INSTRUCTORS
Warm-up Handler and dog zig-zag between the poles as shown in Figure 7-15. Work the dog on both sides and give direction commands at each turn.	**Warm-up** The poles are just markers. Handlers can either go around them or turn in front of them.
Jumping: Send-away to table With dog on the left, do the line of jumps to the table. Repeat rewarding the dog on the table each time. Repeat twice working the dog on the right. With the dog on the left, do the line of jumps to the table. This time keep the dog on the table for a few seconds and then recall over one jump. Praise. Repeat working the dog on the right.	**Jumping: Send-away to table** Check that handlers are using a send-away command as well as a jump command. Bait the table with a toy or tidbit each time. Make sure the handler stands in the centre of the jump when recalling the dog, and that the handler turns the dog on the table to face that jump. It may be necessary to use helpers on either side to make sure that the dog goes over the jump.
See-Saw Review this obstacle, working the dog on both sides. Repeat several times.	**See-Saw** Show handlers how to stop the plank from banging down until the dog learns to control it himself.
Introduce tyre An assistant holds the dog while the handler shows him the hole and calls him through. Repeat. With the dog on the left, the handler encourages him to jump through. Maybe throw a toy through the opening. Repeat working the dog on the right.	**Introduce tyre** Discuss commands: TYRE, HOOP, THROUGH (if not used for the tunnel). At first it may help to use a jump command as well, but this should soon be dropped. Make sure that handlers line the dog up straight.

LESSON 7 • *A Beginner Agility Class*

WORK TO DO	HINTS FOR INSTRUCTORS
Introduce the long jump With the dog on the left, take him over the long jump. Repeat working the dog on the right. Repeat the previous two steps.	**Introduce the long jump** Discuss commands: LONG, RIGHT OVER. Again, it may be help to use the ordinary jump command at first. Make sure the handler turns both ways after the obstacle and not always to the right.
Course Walk the course shown in Figure 7-16 clockwise and then run it with the dog on the left. Walk the course counter-clockwise and then run it with the dog on the right.	**Course** This is the first time the training weaves have been in a course. Reassure handlers that they can use a toy or tidbit for motivation, if necessary. Turn the collapsed tunnel around before running the course counter-clockwise.

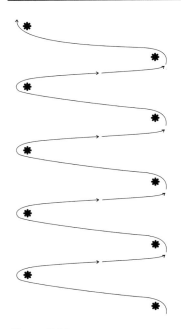

Figure 7-15

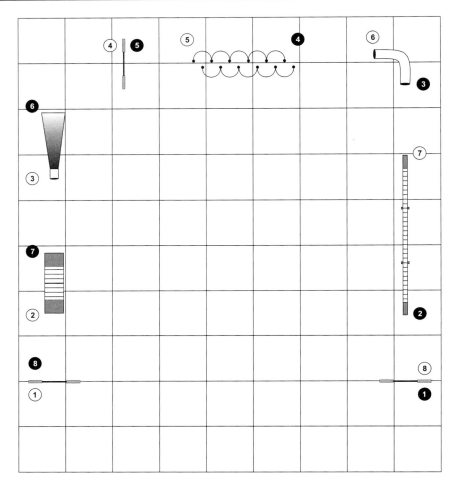

Figure 7-16

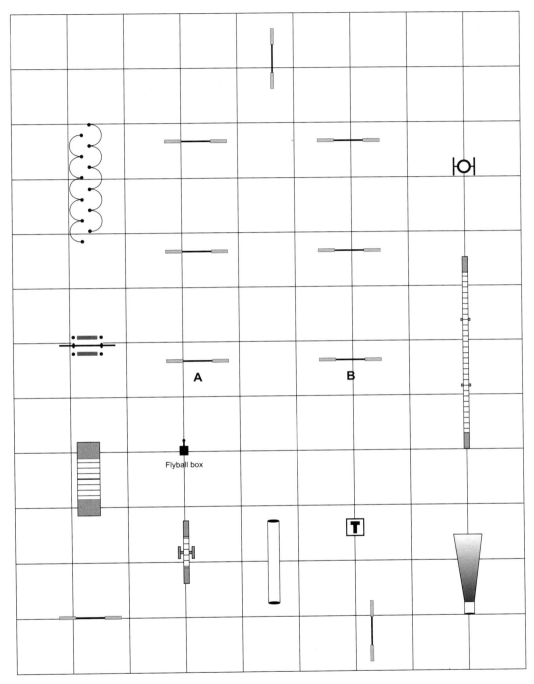

Figure 7-17

LESSON 8
A Beginner Agility Class

Equipment

- Seven hurdles set out in a horseshoe as shown in Figure 7-17

- A-frame, dog walk, see-saw, tyre, mini table, training weave poles, tunnels, long jump and two jumps set out in a course

- Flyball box

LESSON 8 • *A Beginner Agility Class*

WORK TO DO	HINTS FOR INSTRUCTORS
Warm-up With the dog on the left, run in and out of the jumps shown in Figure 7-18. Repeat working the dog on the right.	**Warm-up** Assess handlers control and decide if anyone is ready to try working off lead.
Jumping With the dog on the left, run the sequence shown in Figure 7-18 from A to B. With the dog on the right, run the sequence from B to A. Repeat the previous two steps.	**Jumping** Assess dogs to see if they are ready to jump a little higher. Check handlers and dogs to make sure they are happy on the right. Decide if any dogs are ready to try the exercise off lead.
Flyball Send dog to box from a few yards away.	**Flyball** Assess progress.
Course Walk the course shown in Figure 7-19 several times. Run and enjoy the course! Walk the course in the other direction and run it.	**Course** Set up the course shown in Figure 7-19. Help handlers decide how to handle the course. Give a count on the table and assist at any problem obstacles. Assess progress. Turn the collapsed tunnel and see-saw around and run the course in the opposite direction.

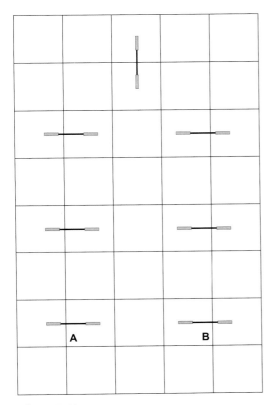

Figure 7-18

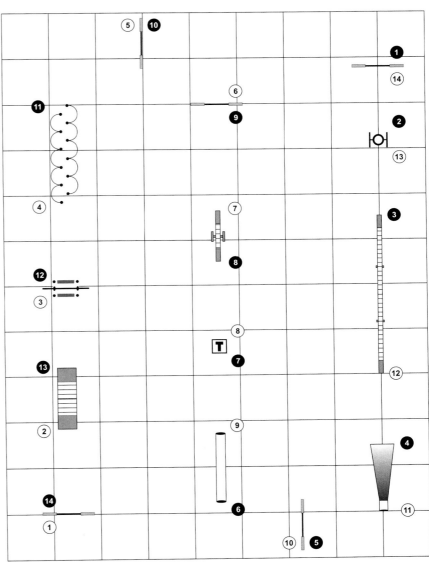

Figure 7-19

Chapter Eight What's Next?

Chapter Eight
What's Next?

One of the difficulties in running Agility classes is that all dogs progress at different rates. Very quickly you find that you have a wide range of abilities within the class.

At the end of any Agility class, *some* of the handlers and dogs will be ready for the next stage. However, other handlers and dogs may need more work at the remedial stages before they are ready to progress further. It is important that handlers are not made to feel like a failure if this is the case. Having a few more weeks of practise at the beginning stages may make all the difference, and get them confident and ready for the next stage of training.

Pushing handlers and dogs on to more challenging and advanced work before they are really ready can cause lots of problems and may even put them off Agility for good.

I hope the reader has found this book useful. Volume III of *Agility Fun The Hobday Way* provides many more lessons for continuing the dog's Agility education. These include lessons on the importance of forward movement, teaching turns, obstacle awareness, and teaching the cross-over.

Other Training Books and Videos by Ruth Hobday

Agility is Fun—Book 1. This book provides a comprehensive step-by-step guide to training a dog for Agility. Fully illustrated, it is suitable for both the beginner and the experienced competitor. Price: £8.00.

Agility is Fun—Book 2. This second book goes into more advanced Agility training. It has a large section on control exercises and a chapter on constructing adjustable height contact obstacles. Price: £10.00.

"Agility is Fun—Take 2". This video demonstrates the exercises for beginner dogs which are covered in Agility is Fun—Book 1. It will help you give your dog a strong basis for future agility accomplishments. Length: 1 hour. Price £20.00.

"Control Exercises". This second video demonstrates some of the control exercises from both books. Length: 30 minutes. Price £17.50.

"Pups Progress". Filmed every two months, this video shows the training of two pups from 6 to 18 months of age. It shows control work taught in a fun way before the pups are old enough to do Agility obstacles, then follows their progress through to their first Agility show. Length: 2 hours. Price: £23.00.

"Problems 1". Problems that a handler may need help overcoming can arise during agility training at any time. The aim of this video is to suggest ideas that may help the handler find a solution to Agility problems without spoiling the dog's enjoyment of the sport. "Problems 1" looks at problems with the contact obstacles, jumps, and the tyre. Length: 1 hour. Price: £20.00.

"Problems 2". This video covers problems with tunnels, weave poles, and the table. It also looks at the behaviour problems that crop up in Agility. Length: 1 hour. Price: £20.00.

"Advanced Control Exercises". This new video demonstrates advanced exercises designed to help tighten up turns and get the dog working at a distance, hopefully enabling the handler to shave vital seconds off their dog's time. Length: 1 hour. Price: £20.00.

"A New Puppy—The Early Days". This video shows the viewer how to teach the very young pup through play. It also shows the socialisation and other experiences that are so vital to a young pup's development. Length: 30 minutes. Price: £16.00.

Ordering Information

Video Format
Prices listed are for PAL video format. For tapes in NTSC format (U.S.), please include an additional £10 per tape.

Postage
For orders in the U.K., add £2 per item.
For orders to Europe, add £3 per item.
For orders to the rest of the world, add £4 per item.

Send orders to:
Hurricane Dog Training
Willow Batch
Carding Mill Valley
Church Stretton
Shropshire, SY6 6JG ENGLAND

Other Publications by Clean Run Productions

Clean Run Magazine

A monthly agility training magazine that features articles by top agility competitors from the U.S. and abroad, training exercises for all levels, courses and course analyses, discussions of rules by judges, handling strategies, discussions of training problems, as well as teaching ideas and plans for instructors. Sample issue: $6. One year subscription: $60 in the U.S., $66 in Canada, $85 Overseas.

Agility Workbook Series

by Clean Run Productions

Each workbook contains exercises and instructional information for an eight-week training program. The Introductory Agility Workbook (132 pp.) is designed for dogs and handlers who do not have any agility training experience. The Intermediate Agility Workbook (122 pp.) builds on this foundation and the Advanced Agility Workbook (136 pp.) provides progressively more difficult exercises to ready handlers for competition. Price: $22 for one book; $20 per book for two or more.

Fundamentals of Course Design for Dog Agility

By Stuart Mah

Whether you're an exhibitor who wants to understand how the design of a course influences the handling decisions you need to make as well as your dog's performance, an instructor who needs to design exercises for a class, an aspiring judge who needs to learn about the elements involved in course design so that you can create realistic and doable courses for competition, or an event organizer who wants to learn about building courses, this book will help you! Price: $26.95.

Ordering Information

Postage

If ordering one book, include $3 shipping for U.S. orders; $5 for Canadian orders; and $9 for Overseas orders. If ordering more than one book, include $2 per book shipping for U.S. orders; $3 per book for Canadian orders; and $7 per book for Overseas orders.

Sales Tax

Mass. residents must include 5% sales tax on merchandise

Payment

Payments must be made in U.S. dollars by check, money order, Visa, or Mastercard.

Send orders to:

Clean Run Productions
35 Walnut Street
Turners Falls, MA 01376-2317
Phone 413-863-9243 or 1-800-311-6503
Fax 413-863-8303
www.cleanrun.com